After Reagan

To David and Danny,
who made the long days worthwhile,
and to Kay,
for her love and understanding.

After Reagan

Confronting
the Changed World Economy

◊

C. Michael Aho
Marc Levinson

Council on Foreign Relations
New York

COUNCIL ON FOREIGN RELATIONS BOOKS

The Council on Foreign Relations, Inc., is a nonprofit and nonpartisan organization devoted to promoting improved understanding of international affairs through the free exchange of ideas. The Council does not take any position on questions of foreign policy and has no affiliation with, and receives no funding from, the United States government.

From time to time, books and monographs written by members of the Council's research staff or visiting fellows, or commissioned by the Council, or written by an independent author with critical review contributed by a Council study or working group are published with the designation "Council on Foreign Relations Book." Any book or monograph bearing that designation is, in the judgment of the Committee on Studies of the Council's board of directors, a responsible treatment of a significant international topic worthy of presentation to the public. All statements of fact and expressions of opinion contained in Council books are, however, the sole responsibility of the author.

Library of Congress Cataloging-in-Publication Data

Aho, C. Michael, 1949-
   After Reagan.

      Includes bibliographies and index.
      1. United States--Economic policy--1981-
      2. United States--foreign economic relations
      3. Capital market. 4. International finance. I. Levinson, Marc.
II. Title.
HC106.8.A36 1988   338.973   88-28514
ISBN 0-87609-040-4
ISBN 0-87609-041-2 (pbk.)

Contents

Foreword

Anthony M. Solomon

What you have before you is an analysis of the critical domestic and international economic choices that will confront the next president in this changed world economy. Allow me to offer first my perspectives.

In January 1989, the next president of the United States will confront a number of old problems in the area of international economic and financial policy that have proved to be complex and intractable, as well as many new ones that will be equally challenging. To say that these will be among the most difficult policy issues that the new administration will face is no exaggeration. Moreover, the substance of the policy analyses and options reviewed as well as decisions the president takes during his early days in office will have great significance, not only for the initial impression he makes on the media and the public, but also for the perceptions of the financial markets and of foreign governments.

To address these problems, in my judgment, the next president's highest priority should be to put together a process of decisionmaking that would be appropriate and rational—and well before the details of the background and policy alternatives of the various issues are considered. Good process leads to better policy decisions. There will always be decisions to make, and policies to implement. What is important is to transcend any particular issue and help to assure that decisions are made on the basis of what is in the long-term interest of the United States, not what is expedient in terms of short-term effects on public opinion or on various constituency groups.

In my experience, spanning half a dozen presidencies, Republican and Democratic alike, this organizational priority was rarely, if ever, recognized and, even when it was, the decisionmaking structures put in place were clumsy, inefficient, or grossly unbalanced.

The basic problem is conceptually very simple. Any new president brings with him to the White House many dedicated, committed partisans whose main—and not inconsiderable—talent has been to get their candidate nominated and then elected. Their loyalty remains if not wholly, still very largely, with the president. And they invariably react to issues, especially complex technical issues, such as the ones characteristic of international economics and finance, from a narrow, domestically oriented political perspective. They have access, trust, and close connections to important constituents and, no less important, contributors. They rarely have expertise in the policy areas where they will be put in the position to render advice. Face it, most of those who join a White House staff are close to being economic illiterates!

Elsewhere in the government, especially in the Treasury, the State Department, and the Office of the U.S. Trade Representative, new appointees put together teams of mostly qualified people drawn from economic careers in the private and public sectors. Those chosen are essentially motivated by the substance of the issues and will formulate policies that they expect the government to pursue. They rarely have domestic political experience. They generally have little regard for the short-term time horizons and the obvious insularity of the political operatives. Often, they are people who are well regarded by influential congressional leaders, at least so long as they are not undercut by the White House staff.

A wise president does well to appreciate the dangers inherent in this configuration of talent versus personal loyalty, and to establish clear lines of authority, communication, policy review mechanisms, and ways of handling internal disagreements long before his administration is faced with a serious test. There are surely various means of achieving what may be called "organized chaos," since no one should be so naive as to believe that policymaking at the highest level of government can ever be made solely with cool, logical, academic detachment. Interests matter. Interests breed emotions. Emotions stand in the way of rational thought, even as they energize the process.

Most of the time, the split between those with the knowledge and competence and those with the direct access to the president, but with too narrow and immediate a focus, is not systematically bridged. An organizational process that takes into account that inevitable split right from the beginning will give the new administration a tremendous leg up in handling what promises to be a daunting array of policy issues soon after the inauguration.

An essential component of this necessary organization should be an economic assistant to the president on the White House staff who is also deputy, and subordinate, to the chairman of the cabinet-level economic policy group, the secretary of the Treasury.

Turning now to the substance of the international economic and financial agenda, as construed in appropriately broad dimensions, it is worthwhile to make a sharp distinction between three classes of problems among the entire array that are bound to be of importance. Nothing could lead to confusion and ineptitude faster than for the new president to react to the varying pressures and end up treating too many international economic problems as equally urgent and equally worthy of his own time. Thus, these distinctions have practical, not just intellectual, relevance.

The first of the three classes includes those problems that require no new initiatives for the time being while the events must be carefully monitored. Here the watchwords are *"do no harm."* Second are those that, in my personal judgment, deserve early and concentrated attention by the president and his administration, because the opportunity is there for meaningful initiatives either to resolve a festering problem or to head off a potentially serious one. This is the class where *"urgent action is required."* And third are those problems that over a period of time will have importance for the nation and its international economic relations, but which are essentially longer term in nature. This is the *"stop and think"* category.

I would put the questions both of foreign investment in the United States and of how to implement the new trade bill in the first class, where the president should endeavor to *do no harm.*

The topic of whether foreign investment in the United States is a good thing has been dintinguished primarily by the lack of appreciation both for the basic economics of the situation and for the facts. Hence, the issue has been raised in the most egregiously xenophobic way, without a sense of balance or historical perspective. The new president will soon learn (if he doesn't know it now) that even with the moderate improvement in the U.S. trade position in 1988, the nation relies on as much as $150 billion a year in foreign capital inflows in order to fill a domestic savings shortfall without stifling domestic investment. Most of those inflows are into financial market instruments that are readily marketable, and thus highly liquid, in response to any concern, real or imagined.

A smaller portion reflects direct foreign investments by foreign countries in U.S. facilities, either through new subsidiaries or through acquisition of existing firms. Those investments not only help finance the U.S. current account deficit. They also bring in new technology, management practices, or export potential. They are not readily liquefied, and, therefore, are not "hot money." They do raise, in some instances, legitimate concerns about national sovereignty, especially in the defense area, but there are existing laws and regulations designed to avoid abuses. The trouble is that some people are convinced, regardless of what the facts may say, that foreign companies seek to operate in the United States, not to make profits but to have a political impact. So, many are calling for restrictions on these foreign investments or ardous reporting requirements that are more intrusive than those faced by U.S. companies abroad.

The topic will tend to run its course and eventually fade out of public discourse (as it did in Europe). The worst thing the next president can do is to try to gain some fleeting political advantage by exploiting the unwarranted fears about the intentions of foreign companies. The best thing he can do is to monitor closely the data, and propose to do nothing about the trend, which is, by and large, good for both the country and the companies involved.

The other area requiring no new initiatives is trade policy. After a massive effort, spanning several years and the scrutiny of dozens of congressional committees, a new trade law came onto the books. It gives substantial new powers to the administration to move in a unilateral and, largely, adversarial direction. The new president should seek to administer the new law fairly, but with regard to the broader economic context, including the impact on consumers, secondary industries, and world trade generally. The initial actions need to be carefully structured to give the appearance of objectivity, rather than of back-door protectionism. If this approach is not followed, substantial harm is likely to result, which will leave everybody worse off. The next president should instead use the authority contained in the new law to support enthusiastically a new round of trade liberalization— one that could eventually take his name—which does promise benefits to all sides.

There is, though, a second class of problems where *urgent action is required.* These will demand presidential leadership and cabinet-level commitment for fashioning new initiatives to come to grips with pressing, long-standing problems that plague the international economy and the world financial system.

To begin with, there is the problem of U.S. fiscal policy. Why is this at the top of an agenda for *international* economic and financial initiatives? Simply because it ultimately has more to do with the balance-of-payments deficit, the value of the dollar, and the competitive position of the United States in world markets than any other single factor. To put it bluntly, until the domestic fiscal position is put in order, U.S. and world financial markets will remain vulnerable to repeated bursts of volatility, similar to and ultimately worse than that we all experienced in October 1987. There can be no stability in exchange markets, bond markets, and stock markets until there is a far better balance between savings and investment in the United States. And the only way to achieve that better balance in the period immediately ahead is through a more disciplined federal government budgetary position.

Second, and closely related, there is a pressing need for better coordination of monetary and fiscal policies among the major industrial countries. Financial markets are useful reference points regarding the appropriateness of economic policies. Left alone, however, financial markets cannot achieve basic economic objectives. That ultimate responsibility rests with governments. And, in an interdependent world, it entails continuing high-level communication and, when feasible, coordination of policies. The results of those efforts will be less instability in financial markets, and a better balance in the pattern of world current account surpluses and deficits. That pays off in less economic dislocation (in the aggregate and in individual industries), in faster rates of sustainable economic growth, and in lower world inflation rates. Every new administration questions the benefits of international policy coordination. That is understandable. But when the alternatives are fairly put before a president, eventually the case is made that we are better off if others are better off and conversely. And that requires differing but compatible policies among the key countries.

Third, and surely also closely related, is the urgent need for coming up with a sensible, credible policy toward short-term movements in the value of the dollar in foreign exchange markets. There is a danger that domestic political instincts will overcome sound analysis, and permit a cynical manipulation of the dollar either through overt actions and statements or through indirection. What we need to hear is a clear statement of what the new administration intends to achieve in macroeconomic policy, and what role the exchange rate will be expected to play in achieving those results, including a viable improvement in the trade deficit.

What I for one would like to hear is a commitment to dollar stability, meaning that the dollar should not become excessively over- or undervalued and that, by and large, its longer-term movements should generally reflect inflation rate differentials between the United States and other key countries. If the monetary and financial authorities of the main industrial countries are in agreement, and take a consistent position toward exchange rate intervention, they can have an over-whelmingly powerful effect on the evolution of market conditions. That insight ought to form the basis for the short-term oriented dollar policy of the next administration, and it ought to be made clear to the markets right at the outset.

Finally, the majority of issues that will confront the next administration in the international economic and financial area are, by my reckoning, to be shunted to the *"think it over"* category. And that includes more than a few questions that others have deemed worthy of urgent action. I am not so sure. I wonder whether any brand new administration can credibly confront problems of some duration with bold new actions and expect, except through sheer luck, to be successful where others have been mired in protracted frustration.

First is the developing country debt predicament. Since the outset, experts have been coming up, to no avail, with grand schemes to resolve the problem once and for all. Few have had merit. Many ideas have been suggested. Those that have been tried have sometimes made a modest contribution, and have been rarely more than a footnote to the main story: generating policy reform in the debtor nations, while holding out the hope for eventual economic progress as those reforms take effect. Although it will be essential for the United States to supply political leadership in mobilizing some degree of official support for debt reduction policies, practicality will require a greater willingness to compromise on the part of the key players than we have seen to date. The new president ought to revisit the topic, listen to the experts, and discuss the issues with other government leaders, including the heads of the key debtor countries—at least one of which will be equally new on the job (Mr. Salinas of Mexico)—before making his move.

Second is the problem of burden-sharing for the common defense. The United States needs to reduce the fiscal deficit. A good part of that spending is to support U.S. forces abroad. Why not have the allies pay more? My advice is to go slow. The facts are less than clear-cut regarding the true relative burdens and the possible savings for the United States. And the political and psychological stakes are high. If the United States is perceived as acting unilaterally and in its own narrow interest, the fallout could be highly adverse to the entire defense strategy. This is an area in which it is easy to be penny wise, pound foolish. It would be better to come up with a well thought out and carefully crafted approach, targeted to each ally individually, which would allow them to take on specific tactical responsibilities while leaving the basic strategic responsibility with the United States. Naturally, such an approach cannot be forged overnight; time needs to be taken to assure that something more valuable than budgetary expenditure is not lost, namely the alliance itself.

A third area where the president ought to stop and think is longer-run energy policy. Aside from the immediate role energy taxes may play in righting our fiscal situation, there are diverse views on long-run policies. I would urge caution. The oil market is volatile, and a hasty U.S. initiative could be perilous, not least for some important developing countries who are dependent on oil exports for their very survival. It would be worthwhile to develop a coherent long-term energy policy, but it is not an urgent need early in the next administration.

Finally, there is a small but vocal band of commentators, plus some political figures, who are calling for grand reform of the international monetary system. Proposals have been made for reestablishing some form of fixed exchange rates for the dollar, or even putting gold back into the system. Lately, the interest has turned to prudential matters, such as international harmonization of regulations for securities markets to prevent a repeat of the October 1987 stock market crash.

My recommendation is that the new administration should leave the debate on these topics to academics, think tanks, and regulatory agencies for the time being. Eventually, they will be live issues. After all, the reconstitution of the European Community in the 1990s also calls for a thoughtful (but not pressing) U.S. response, one more carefully considered than that which has come from Washington so far.

But these grander topics are not handled well in an atmosphere of urgency. Contemplation and analysis are more appropriate, and I would imagine that a new administration faced with far more pressing concerns will agree.

In summary, the international economic and financial agenda is long, complicated, and intertwined with important domestic issues. The highest priority for the next president is to put in place a rational and responsible process for decisionmaking, so that the steps finally taken will have been crafted with competence and long-term insight. Structuring organizations appropriately, including the cabinet, its committees and working groups, and the other vehicles for melding the various components of the government that must contribute to any important international initiative, is not a glamourous or headline-grabbing endeavor. Unless it is done consciously and conscientiously, however, I would seriously doubt that the next administration will be any more prepared to deal skillfully, or at least competently, with the burdens of a complex and interrelated world economy and financial system than were any of its predecessors.

I had the privilege to chair the Council on Foreign Relations study group (members listed on page 233) that examined these issues at length. What follows is the product of those sessions, and I highly recommend it to you.

Anthony M. Solomon is currently chairman of S.G. Warburg (U.S.A.), Inc. He was formerly the assistant secretary of state for economic affairs, undersecretary for monetary affairs to the U.S. Treasury Department, and president of the Federal Reserve Bank of New York.

Preface

We don't envy the next president. Whoever takes over after Ronald Reagan will face different constraints and more difficult choices and challenges in dealing with the global economy than any of his predecessors. His success in managing international economic issues, while avoiding undesirable consequences for American living standards, will go a long way to determine his reelection prospects four years hence. He must be prepared for constant engagement with other countries, the Congress, and the American public, because if one international economic issue recedes from view, it is likely to be replaced by another. If the next president ignores the global economy, he does so at his peril.

This book provides an introduction to the international economic challenges and choices that will confront the next president. It is not written for the experts—although we hope they will find new insights here—but for a much wider audience for whom an understanding of international economic issues is vital to making each day's government and business decisions.

The first lesson an author on this subject must learn is that in today's integrated, interdependent economy, it is hard to draw the line between domestic and international economic issues. The domestic U.S. budget deficit clearly has international economic consequences, and we treat it extensively; but, despite each having working spouses and two children under the age of six, we felt that child care had less of an international dimension. (Although, we did think about it.) Some potential economic developments are also not treated in full. Economic reform in China and the Soviet Union could, some years hence, significantly affect the global economy, but it is only dealt with under other issues rather than as a separate topic. Similarly, energy policy that possessed overwhelming importance when Ronald Reagan came into office appears less earthshattering today. It is addressed in an ancillary way, as an option for raising revenue through increased gasoline taxes, or as an oil import fee. We felt it difficult to predict when the oil cartel might be successful in raising prices. If oil prices do jump sharply, however, as they did in 1973 and 1979, most of the problems described in the following pages would be exacerbated and the case for international cooperation and coordination would be even stronger.

This book is not intended as a blueprint of what the next president should do in the first ninety days after inauguration. Rather, it examines those issues that we feel should be accorded priority attention over the next four years, both in light of how the world economy has changed and in light of the legacy being left by the Reagan presidency. Some, such as the budget deficit, will require the immediate attention of the president. Others, like foreign investment, financial market regulation, and labor adjustment policy, require only general presidential support and staff attention at a lower level, in anticipation that at any time they might emerge onto the front pages.

After Reagan grew out of a Council on Foreign Relations study group on the Economic Choices Confronting the Next President, which met four times between March and June 1988. It was chaired by Anthony M. Solomon. He generously shared his time in planning the meetings, and, drawing upon his vast experience in making economic policy, he guided our discussions with intelligence and skill, always ensuring that the group did not stray far from the subject matter at hand. The members of the study group are listed on page 233, and we are pleased that eight of them were willing to set down on paper their own priorities and prescriptions for the next president. Those pieces begin on page 191.

We are indebted to many people who helped at various stages in the production of this book. Tom Bayard, Lindley Clark, Richard Gardner, William Gleysteen, Bob Hormats, Kent Hughes, Shafiqul Islam, Michael Mandelbaum, Dorothy Sobol, and Bruce Stokes read the entire manuscript and participated in an author's review group, very ably chaired by William Diebold. We benefited a great deal from those discussions. William Diebold, Shafiqul Islam, and Roger Kubarych made valuable comments on separate chapters on other occasions. In addition to the members of the study group, several other people provided insights along the way including Jonathan Aronson, Marshall Carter, Christine Cumming, Richard Feinberg, Geza Feketekuty, Alton Frye, Gary Horlick, Merit Janow, Abe Katz, Richard McGahey, Hugh Patrick, Andrew Pierre, Alan Romberg, Susan Schwab, Greg Treverton, William N. Walker, and Georgios Zavvos. Many thanks to all of them. Although we benefited from their input, the text before you is our own, and no one else is at fault.

At the Council, we greatly appreciate the unwavering support given by Peter Tarnoff, president, William Gleysteen, vice president of studies, and David Kellogg, director of publications, throughout the entire effort. Every author should enjoy such excellent top-level encouragement and help. Stephanie Hoelscher served conscientiously as the rapporteur for the study group and diligently handled all administrative issues, including the initial typing of the manuscript. After she left to return to graduate school, Dorothy Price picked up right where Stephanie had left off, and got a quick taste of what it is like when two anxious authors are trying to finish a book. Above all, Suzanne Hooper, assistant director of the Council's International Trade Project, read, reread, edited, and commented continuously upon the book, probably suffering a deterioration in her social life as a consequence. *After Reagan* would not have appeared until long after Reagan without her initiative, perseverance, and dedication. We bet she is glad this book is done.

On behalf of the Council, we would like to thank General Motors and the Rockefeller Foundation for their generous support of the International Trade Project, from which this is the fourth publication. We also gratefully acknowledge the support of the Hochschild Fund in making possible an in-depth review of the draft manuscript of this volume. The Hochschild Fund was created by the contributions of the AMAX Foundation and the family and friends of Walter Hochschild, a member of the Council from 1947 until his death in 1983.

Finally, this book would not have been possible without the constant support of our wives, Amy and Kay. That support is appreciated more than they realize. Because their future is at stake, Aho dedicates this book to David and Danny, who make the long days worthwhile, and Levinson dedicates it to Kay, for her love and understanding.

C. Michael Aho
Marc Levinson

August 1988

After Reagan

1

The Challenge

The 1988 presidential election marks a new stage for the U.S. economy. Whoever moves into the White House on January 20, 1989, will confront international economic challenges unlike those faced by any of his predecessors. Issues long considered so arcane that the president rarely paused to think of them—exchange rates, trade rules, foreign investment, international coordination of tax and budget policies—will be in an unaccustomed place at the top of the political agenda. To govern successfully, the president will be forced to come to grips with subjects that those in office before him, by and large, have been content to leave to the technicians. The disinterest in the international economic dimension expressed so succinctly in President Richard Nixon's 1972 statement "I don't give a #&?§ about the lira" recorded for all eternity on the Watergate tapes, is inconceivable in 1989.

In the past, save in rare moments of crisis, presidents have been able to deal with foreign economic policy at their leisure. They have made full use of that ability, since improvements in exchange rate arrangements and revisions in foreign aid programs are not normally the sorts of things for which voters are likely to express their thanks at the polls. In 1989, however, the new president will not have the option of focusing on social welfare programs or military preparedness, while putting the global economy on the back burner. As a perceptive student of the presidency recently observed, "The world is closing in on the White House."[1] And, since the president will need the cooperation of Congress to steer a new international economic course, it could just as easily be said that the world is closing in on both ends of Pennsylvania Avenue.

The growing interdependence of the world economy poses severe risks for the U.S. economy in the next few years. A collapse of the dollar, driven by a loss of investor confidence and capital flight, could force interest rates sharply higher and send the United States into a deep recession, even as the unfavorable exchange rate requires America to produce more for each Japanese computer or German car it wants to buy. The default of a developing country with tens of billions of dollars of foreign debts could threaten the survival of major U.S. banks, and with them the world banking system. Financial market instability abroad can be transferred to markets in New York and Chicago in an instant. International trade, which has contributed so heavily to improved economic welfare since World War II, could diminish as one nation after another acts to protect its industries at the expense of others.

And even if none of these cataclysmic events comes to pass, major international economic initiatives will be required to avert a decline in living standards in the United States. The danger that Americans will be less well off, on average, in 1992 than they are today is quite real. That alone makes it a political necessity for the next administration to give global economic relations an unaccustomed priority.

Has the world changed that much? Indeed it has. The eight years of Ronald Reagan's presidency have witnessed two fundamental shifts in the world economy, shifts that began long before President Reagan took office in 1981 but that have accelerated sharply under his administration. One is the rapid internationalization of capital markets. The other is the widespread acknowledgment that America's international economic dominance is not as great as it had been for most of the period since World War II. In combination, these two factors will significantly limit the choices and options available to the next president.

And they will impinge severely upon policies far removed from the economic realm. The ability to reshape defense strategy, social welfare programs, education, and business regulation will be constrained by international economic factors far more than ever before. The neat divisions on the government's organization chart, which leave security matters to the Pentagon and energy policy to the Energy Department, are eroding rapidly. As demands of foreign creditors for a return on their capital become a paramount consideration in Washington, tight domestic budgets and the need to run a trade surplus will ensure that no part of the government will be able to operate as freely as it did in times of greater economic independence.

Capital Constraints

Capital markets have always had an international aspect, of course; international bank lending is as old as the banking business itself. In the 1960s, banks began making dollar-denominated loans from loosely regulated foreign branches in what became known as the Eurodollar market, and lending to the governments of developing countries changed from a sideline into a major business. But not until high-speed computer and communications technology came into wide use during the 1980s did each nation's separate securities and banking industries coalesce into a single worldwide financial market in which political boundaries have almost ceased to have meaning.

In this new financial world, investors in Zurich or Auckland can buy the stock of American corporations listed on exchanges in Frankfurt or Tokyo, can hedge against a fall in the price of their shares by acquiring stock options in Philadelphia, and can then minimize their exposure to changes in the value of the dollar by selling exchange rate futures contracts in London or Chicago—all in a matter of seconds, without moving from their computer terminals. They can execute, or even program their computers to execute, complex international arbitrage strategies, buying in one market and almost simultaneously selling in another market halfway around the globe to capture a momentary divergence in prices.

Borrowers can do much the same. If dealing with their local banker no longer suits their needs, companies can raise dollars from a Japanese bank in California or yen from a British bank in Paris. If the bond market in New York looks unappealing, they can obtain British pounds on the market for short-term commercial paper in London and then swap repayment obligations with another debtor who owes U.S. dollars but would rather make monthly payments in sterling. And if all else fails, well, there are always "junk bonds," securities backed with little more than a promise of future growth that someone may be willing to buy if the interest rate is high enough.

Where these largely electronic transactions occur makes little difference to investors, to borrowers, or to their computers. Capital has ceased to have national characteristics, and national capital markets are no longer identifiably separate and distinct. To speak of "American capital" and "foreign investment" as discrete sums of money with differing attributes is to seriously misunderstand the modern world.

An integral part of the new global financial market is currency trading. The equivalent of well over $300 billion dollars was changed from one currency to another on the average day in 1987. Some of this activity, to be sure, can be attributed to tourists stocking up on francs for their next trip to Paris or to importers needing to pay for merchandise ordered from abroad. The vast majority, however, has no immediate relationship to international travel or trade. Computers have made speculative currency dealing into a big, if risky, business in which banks, brokerage houses, and multinational corporations participate day in, day out. Although the profit on any given trade is likely to be tiny, electronic tools give traders the ability to buy and sell a thousand times a day, dealing millions of dollars with nothing more than a keystroke.

The unregulated markets in foreign exchange have a direct effect on the interest rates paid by every American, thanks to the enormous amount of foreign investment in the U.S. economy. As the U.S. government has run unprecedented budget deficits totaling $1.3 trillion over the past seven years, it has relied heavily on foreigners to provide the capital it needs to operate. At the end of 1987, an estimated $290 billion of U.S. Treasury securities were in foreign hands, as well as $171 billion in corporate bonds, $540 billion in bank deposits, and $261 billion in direct investment. For the most part, these investments are passive. Their owners have no particular desire to own *American* debt; they have placed their money here only because, for the moment, this is where they can earn the greatest return, given the amount of risk they are prepared to tolerate. Exchange rate fluctuations, however, may throw that return into doubt. Dollar-denominated U.S. Treasury bonds in New York must pay more than West German government bonds in Frankfurt if investors expect the dollar to fall against the deutsche mark; if the difference in interest is not sufficient to cover the expected change in exchange rates, investors of all nationalities will sell their U.S. holdings and take their money elsewhere. Home mortgages in Dallas, auto financing in Minneapolis, and small business loans in Los Angeles will become more costly as a result.

The unpredictable ebb and flow of cash poses limits on the ability of the leader of any nation, including the president of the United States, to direct the domestic economy. This does not come as news to many countries, including some industrialized nations, in which international capital flows have long been a matter of course; they are already cognizant of the difficulties of shaping economic policy alone. However, for the United States, which is proud of its supposed economic autonomy, the idea that the cooperation of others is required to direct the economy is novel—and uncomfortable.

In an economy relatively open to the world, as the American economy increasingly is, the traditional instruments of economic policy are blunted. Managing the money supply to regulate interest rates while allowing the economy room to expand is immensely more difficult than it was in the past, because huge sums of money in search of the most profitable home may suddenly wash onto American shores, driving interest rates lower, or may just as suddenly flee for more profitable investments abroad, forcing up the cost of borrowing. Fiscal measures—spending and tax policies—are also harder to manipulate. Back when international capital flows were smaller and slower, a boost in government spending was sure to put money in consumers' pockets and trigger a boom, at least temporarily. But in an economy wide open to the world, this may not happen: rising interest rates may drive up the country's currency so rapidly that imports surge and exports collapse, nullifying the government's expansionary intent. Economists remain woefully unable to predict how exchange rates will react to such economic policy changes. To a far greater extent than in the past, the individuals who must make the difficult economic choices in Washington are in the dark.

From the vast global community of investors, the policy pronouncements of government officials receive an instantaneous and critically important verdict. A president must face the voters only once in four years, but he must face the judgment of the markets every business day. That undefinable thing called "market confidence" has very real and very major effects on the nation's economy: if "the markets" do not believe that the nation's economic policy is sound, traders have the ability to drive the dollar to the astronomical heights it attained in 1984, or to send it tumbling in near panic, as they did in 1987. Funds may flow in from abroad or just as quickly flow out as investors' assessments change, lowering or raising domestic interest rates in the process. Governments and central banks may attempt to stem the market's tide, as they did by spending billions of yen, marks, and pounds to stabilize the American dollar in 1987 and 1988, but such a government-sponsored effort is impossible to sustain if it runs counter to the views of private investors whose combined resources are far larger. The next president may be able to score points with the voters by railing against Wall Street speculators and avaricious foreign bankers, but he will not be able to keep the economy on course without their constant help.

Dominance on the Wane

The other development that will serve to limit the next president's economic choices is the relative decline of the international economic position of the United States. That relative decline is a long-standing trend, and is not necessarily a cause for worry. Yet for a nation accustomed to thinking of itself as the world's undisputed economic leader, able to do as it chooses without relying on the support of others, the transformation from being the world's largest creditor to being the world's largest debtor during the Reagan years has required an uneasy adjustment to the notion that the United States no longer possesses the power always to have its own way. Even as it is less able to take the lead in resolving international economic and political problems, the United States is also less willing to do so, as Americans become more reluctant to foot the bill.

America's economic decline, it should be emphasized, is only relative, not absolute. The United States is not becoming poorer, and its economy is not weak or feeble. America's farms, mines, factories, and offices produced $4.5 trillion of goods and services in 1987, far surpassing second-place Japan's $2 trillion. That total assures that, just as his predecessors did, the next president will have more influence on economic matters than any other world leader. But the United States has ceased to dominate the world economy in the way it did for nearly four decades after World War II. As a result, the president is no longer the all-powerful economic head of the industrialized world. His leadership is subject to question and challenge. Now, and for the foreseeable future, he is only first among a group of increasingly assertive equals. He can persuade, but he is less and less able to demand that other nations act as America desires.

Although this change of position has been gradual, it has been developing ever since the early 1950s, when the United States, its farms and factories undamaged by World War II, was indisputably at the center of the world economy. In 1950, with Europe and Japan still in the early stages of postwar reconstruction, it produced 40 percent of the economic output of the entire world. Americans enjoyed an average income of $1,501, the average Briton $744, the average Frenchman $684, the average German $490, and the average Japanese less than $250. America's prosperity enabled it to contribute $17.1 billion—the equivalent of $87 billion at 1988 prices—in nonmilitary aid to other countries between 1946 and 1950, plus $9.4 billion in loans and considerable military assistance. Other nations' reliance on America's money and its military might put them in a poor position to oppose U.S. policies.

Under those circumstances, when the president of the United States talked, leaders of nations with market economies had little choice but to listen. At the Bretton Woods conference in 1944, convened to restructure the world economy in the aftermath of the Great Depression and World War II, delegates from forty-four nations largely accepted American proposals. And, in a symbolic move, the two major economic institutions created at Bretton Woods, the International Monetary Fund and the World Bank, both built headquarters in Washington, D.C., three blocks from the White House.

As a result of decisions at Bretton Woods, the U.S. dollar became the keystone of a system of stable exchange rates, forcing other countries to make economic adjustments in order to keep the value of their currencies in line while allowing the United States to satisfy foreigners' economic claims simply by printing more money. American ideas about international trade, including the basic belief that a single set of rules should govern trade between all countries, became the fundamental building blocks of international commerce. American insistence on a free flow of foreign investment meant that American companies, armed with valuable dollars, were able to acquire new subsidiaries on every continent, while corporations based in Europe and Japan lacked the foreign exchange to do likewise in the United States. The president's freedom of action was so great that as late as 1971, President Nixon was able to unilaterally withdraw the long-standing American promise to exchange dollars for gold. U.S. trading partners, who had been willing to accumulate large amounts of dollars because of America's pledge to back them with gold, were not consulted.

It was the move to freely floating exchange rates in 1973 and the trade boycott by petroleum-exporting countries the same year that made most Americans realize that other countries were claiming for themselves a greater say-so in world economic affairs. But accepting their right to participate in making economic policy has not come easily. The attitude that America is different from other countries, independent and self-sufficient, remains unyielding.

Signs that this attitude no longer corresponds to reality became evident during the 1980s. When huge budget deficits pushed interest rates far above the rate of inflation, causing the dollar to soar and leading to record trade deficits, U.S. demands that other countries stimulate their economies to accept more imports met resistance from foreign officials who said bluntly that it was America's turn to adjust. When bank loans to developing countries began turning sour in 1982, threatening the stability of the entire banking system, U.S. officials found themselves largely powerless to correct the situation, let alone to provide the financial aid Latin American countries needed to get their economies back on track. When other countries' barriers to U.S. exports emerged as a major political issue in the United States in 1984, America's international influence was not enough to reverse the worldwide trend toward protectionism. Indeed, the response preferred by many in Congress was to close U.S. markets.

An equally important and emotionally wrenching aspect of the relative decline of American power is the growing gap between the country's long-standing international security commitments and its ability or at least its willingness to pay for them. Its military strength, perhaps as much as its economic strength, has been critical to America's ability to maintain its position as a dominant power. While that dominance remains, financial realities in the United States, as well as a growing political opinion that prosperous allies should bear a greater share of common defense burdens, will force unpleasant choices about how defense commitments are to be met, or whether military deployments must be scaled back. A reduction of the U.S. contribution to the defense of Western Europe and the Pacific, however, would be accompanied by a further lessening of U.S. influence, perhaps reflected in an even weaker ability to gain concessions in the economic sphere.[2]

The next president will have to face the effects of America's relative decline from the day he takes office. Other industrial countries—West Germany, Switzerland, Japan, Belgium—now have living standards equal to or greater than those in the United States, and they demand treatment as equals. Americans trail citizens of Japan, Switzerland, and several other nations in per-capita income. Foreigners now have more money invested in the U.S. economy than Americans have invested abroad, and their banks have replaced U.S. banks as the world's largest. Their companies have a high degree of technological sophistication, and are able to control access to sophisticated products and processes that the United States needs to prosper. Moreover, they have trade surpluses with the United States that added up to a record $171 billion in 1987.[3] In facing the economic challenges the 1990s will bring, challenges that the growing internationalization of the world economy has placed beyond the ability of any one nation to resolve, the next president will continually be required to seek the cooperation of other nations and accommodate their desires. Gaining that cooperation will not be easy: despite their admiration of the rapid rate of job creation in the United States, many foreign leaders feel they have exercised far more prudent economic stewardship than recent U.S. presidents, suggesting that perhaps American leaders have a thing or two to learn from them, as well as the other way around.

The New Realities

Because of the internationalization of capital markets and the increasing economic power of foreign nations, which will diminish the next president's ability to exert a strong hand in relations with other countries, he will face difficult economic challenges—challenges far different from those that have greeted almost every other president since World War II. High inflation, high unemployment, or both, confronted most recent presidents, and Ronald Reagan, who was first elected in a year in which consumer prices rose 13.5 percent and unemployment averaged 7.1 percent, was no exception. Although current economic indicators are better, there remains a danger that resurgent inflation will force up interest rates, confronting the newly elected president with an economic downturn that would severely constrain his ability to propose new programs and policies. He will also have to oversee a major reorientation of the U.S. economy. For the past several years the United States has consumed more than it has produced by borrowing from abroad. In the future, the United States will have to produce more than it consumes in order to service those debts.

The next president, then, faces a serious risk that he will preside over a deterioration of America's standard of living. Avoiding lower living standards will be difficult, in good part because the American political system tends to be preoccupied with crises of the moment and to postpone dealing with less-pressing concerns until an immediate government response is required. But the problems that could lead to slower economic growth or even to economic decline are already visible. Addressing them will require astute and creative leadership.

Large budget deficits will narrow the new president's latitude to propose new programs, as spending constraints will require growth in any one budget area to be offset by retrenchment in others. They will also inhibit the use of expansionary fiscal policy as a means of combating recession, since increased U.S. government spending will only worsen the world's economic imbalances. Improvements in economic welfare will have to come from market-driven economic growth, not from tax cuts or additional government spending.

In addition, relations between the administration and Congress promise to be contentious. Congress, severely neglected in the formulation of international economic policy during the Reagan administration, is not inclined to grant a new president blanket approval to negotiate trade agreements, new international monetary arrangements, or broad authority to cut government spending. Yet even as members of Congress vigorously question whether the United States can bear the high cost of world leadership in economic and security affairs, Congress is ill equipped to systematically analyze foreign policy trade-offs and is inherently more sympathetic to nationalist or isolationist sentiments than is the executive branch. Engaging Congress constructively in shaping America's international economic policy will be a challenge of the first order.

Five new economic realities will dominate American political life in the 1990s. One will be an *enormous debt obligation to foreigners*. The level of the federal government's total debt is not the problem; there are many foreign countries in which the government's accumulated debt represents a higher share of economic output than is the case in the United States. The problem is that the United States does not save enough and many of the creditors are now foreign citizens. Much of their investment—over $400 billion net by mid-1988—is in the form of government bonds that require fixed annual debt service. Private companies have borrowed heavily abroad as well, increasing the nation's foreign repayment obligations still more. Most of that debt, to be sure, is owed in American dollars, but the consequences will be unpleasant if the U.S. government attempts to deal with it by inflating away its value. There are only two other options, aside from defaulting on the debt. One is for Americans to consume less, to lower their standards of living, in order that some of the goods they are now consuming can be given to foreign creditors. The other is to increase the productivity of the U.S. economy, so there will be more goods available to trade to foreigners without reducing the amount Americans are able to enjoy.

Productivity—the amount of economic wealth produced by the economy for each hour of labor, dollar of capital, and pound of natural resources—has risen slowly in recent years. One reason for the trend is that a growing share of Americans are employed in service industries, where productivity gains are generally harder to come by than in manufacturing. A more important cause, however, has been the reluctance of companies, whether American-owned or foreign, to invest in state-of-the-art facilities in this country rather than overseas. The surplus capacity in U.S. manufacturing until 1988 discouraged construction of new plants and equipment. Then, too, such newly industrializing nations as Taiwan, Korea, Mexico, and Brazil are in direct competition with the United States for certain types of investment. These nations often have access to the latest in manufacturing technology and to lower labor costs as well; the decision to erect a new steel plant in Indiana or a chemical plant in Texas is, in essence, a long-term gamble that some developing country will not build a plant capable of matching American quality at lower cost, forcing down prices around the world and rendering the investment unprofitable.

Another economic reality of the 1990s will be *intense concern about the patterns of international trade*. Protectionism and demands for greater access to foreign markets are and will continue to be potent political issues in the United States, driven by huge trade deficits that will not disappear overnight. Even if the lower dollar turns the U.S. trade deficit into a surplus, individual industries threatened by low-wage or subsidized competition, from garment makers to airplane manufacturers, will continue to clamor for restrictions on imports. As the U.S. trade balance improves, those of the West European and East Asian countries will deteriorate, leading to greater protectionist pressures abroad. The president will need to search for new international arrangements—be they treaties with individual countries or a new multilateral agreement among the ninety-six members of the General Agreement on Tariffs and Trade—that will keep trade flowing relatively freely and allow a continuation of the great increase in international commerce that has been critical to the world's economic growth since 1945.

The growing importance of relatively new players in the world economy will greatly complicate the new president's task. Taiwan, accorded diplomatic recognition by only a handful of nations, has run trade surpluses so consistently that it has displaced West Germany as the possessor of the world's largest foreign exchange reserves, with more than $85 billion of gold and foreign currencies in its vaults. The Republic of Korea, until recently known primarily for its textiles and apparel, has emerged as a major exporter of sophisticated manufactures, from automobiles to computer chips. The export-driven growth of both countries, and the deliberate undervaluation of their currencies to maintain large trade surpluses, will continue to cause delicate economic problems for the United States. The Koreans in particular are likely to assume a greater role in world economic affairs. In addition, the People's Republic of China has already become a leading international competitor in textile and apparel manufacturing and shipbuilding, and its almost unlimited supply of labor gives it the ability to swamp the industrialized world with low-cost manufactured goods. Integrating it into the world economy in an orderly way will be an ongoing challenge.

Improving the trade situation also means taking initiatives to deal with the massive foreign debt overhanging much of the developing world. Developing nations now owe in excess of $1.2 trillion to foreign banks, foreign governments, and international lending agencies. Short of a large rise in the prices of the commodities they produce, nothing save a reduction in their debt service will enable such erstwhile customers as Brazil, Mexico, and Venezuela to become large buyers of American products once again. To date, banks have set aside reserves against some of their foreign loans, but, by and large, debtor countries' requirements for dollars with which to make quarterly interest payments have not been reduced. Latin America remains so saddled with debt service that standards of living are falling, a situation that not only dries up export markets but also exacerbates the problem of illegal migration to the United States—and threatens the political stability of the countries involved. Alleviating the debt situation is likely also to require defining new roles for the International Monetary Fund, the World Bank, the Inter-American Development Bank, and other international institutions that the United States has long supported, but toward which American public opinion has become increasingly hostile in recent years.

A third economic reality of the 1990s is *the need for international cooperation in regulating financial markets*. A decade ago, this would have appeared on almost no one's list of major economic policy issues. But as the banking, insurance, and securities industries have become truly international in scope, individual players increasingly have been able to avoid national rules designed to protect the safety and soundness of the financial system by moving their transactions to another country with less-stringent regulations. It is not enough to prohibit stock trading based on undisclosed "inside information" in New York when many of the same stocks are listed in Tokyo, where insider trading has never been punished. Requiring companies to disclose far more information before selling securities in the United States than they must reveal in Europe serves to push business offshore.

Harmonizing banking and securities regulations around the world is the only way to resolve these conflicts. The first tentative steps have been taken in the banking field, and the stock market crash of October 19–20, 1987—which resulted in a three-day halt to all stock trading in Hong Kong, the temporary suspension of trading in some stocks in New York, and the interruption of stock index futures trading in Chicago—gave impetus to the search for similar accords in the securities area. Politically, harmonizing regulation is likely to pose difficulties, because it will require national governments to surrender some of their autonomy in the regulatory area. Creating the pressure for movement in that direction will be one of the next president's tasks, albeit one that is sure to win few votes from an electorate that cannot begin to comprehend the technical issues involved.

The fourth major economic reality will be *a large and growing level of foreign ownership of America's productive base*. This is an emotionally charged issue for many Americans, with some members of Congress demanding restrictions on foreign investment or mandatory registration of foreign investors even as governors compete to attract investment to their states. With the dollar sinking to low levels in order to bring U.S. trade into balance or even surplus, dollar-denominated stocks will continue to look cheap to investors with pockets full of marks, pounds, or yen, and American real estate appears similarly attractive. It will be awkward for the United States, which has long urged other countries to eliminate their barriers to foreign investment, to erect barriers of its own, and it is unclear what benefits those barriers might bring. The growing diversity of international business arrangements, including joint ventures, and licensing arrangements, makes the idea of policies to benefit U.S. companies archaic. But calls for tighter controls on foreigners who want to buy into America are likely to become a long-term feature of the political landscape.

The final new reality is *the need for the world's major economic powers to cooperate in making economic policy*. This idea hardly seems novel, yet the notion that heads of government, ministers of finance, and central bank presidents should regularly convene to seek common ground in dealing with their economies is relatively new. This cooperation, whether in the form of explicit joint decisions about what steps each country will take or in the form of independent actions of individual countries taken after consultation with trading partners, must go far beyond monetary policy moves and budget matters. In a relatively open world economy, for example, taxes have emerged quite unintentionally as a subject of coordination: the massive U.S. personal and corporate income tax restructurings of 1981 and 1986 effectively forced other countries to undertake tax reform of their own.[4] Matters such as the size of the budget, the scope of defense spending, the desirability of taxing imported oil, and the structure of agricultural subsidies will all be on the international bargaining table. Coordination will grow from something that happens at annual summit meetings to an ongoing part of running a government, including the government of the United States. The fact that different countries have differing preferences, priorities, and understandings of how economies function will cause coordination to become a standing source of international contention.

All of these realities will limit the new president's options in the world economy of the 1990s, even as the rapid pace of technological advance makes people ever more concerned about the consequences of economic change. Advances in microelectronics, enhanced telecommunications, biotechnical discoveries, and other developments will continue to reshape the world economy. They have already made many of the existing political institutions, laws, and ways of thinking about economic issues obsolete.[5] Rapid change is difficult to accept under the best of conditions. If Americans find their economic circumstances worsening rather than improving, they are likely to lash out at the remote forces they do not understand, but that they hold to blame for the decline. The national mood would call for turning inward, in a direction that can only diminish the nation's economic well-being.

The United States is becoming less important in the world economy even as the world economy is becoming more important for the United States. If Americans are to be better off at the end of the next decade than they were at the beginning, it will be incumbent upon the new president to make uncomfortable and unpopular choices in recognition of that fact.

Finding a new role in the international economy will require far more than passing new laws or calling upon the aid of international organizations. There are no easy answers or simple slogans. By and large, the very structures that are needed to deal with the new economic realities either are in disarray or do not exist at all. Yet there is no alternative. Failing to address the new economic realities is a certain path to economic decline. Helping America rise to the challenge will be the urgent task for the president who comes after Reagan.

Notes

1. Richard Rose, *The Post-Modern President: The White House Meets the World* (London: Chatham House, 1988).
2. Samuel P. Huntington, "Coping with the Lippmann Gap," *Foreign Affairs*, vol. 66, no. 3 (Winter 1988), pp. 454–77. David P. Calleo, Harold van B. Cleveland and Leonard Silk, "The Dollar and the Defense of the West," *Foreign Affairs*, vol. 66, no. 4 (Spring 1988), pp. 846–62.
3. This number includes the value of the exports while imports include the cost of insurance and freight for imported merchandise.
4. Joseph Pechman, ed., *World Tax Reform* (Washington, D.C.: Brookings Institution, 1988).
5. W. Michael Blumenthal, "The World Economy and Technological Change," *Foreign Affairs*, vol. 66, no. 3 (Winter 1988), pp. 529–50.

2

Macroeconomic Maladies

The biggest international economic challenge facing the next president will be the elimination of the global trade and financial imbalances without causing a worldwide recession. The next four years will be a transition period for the world economy as today's massive imbalances are eliminated. The record U.S. trade deficit will move toward or into surplus in order to service mounting foreign debt, but how? Which other countries are willing to accept trade deficits in order to accommodate a U.S. surplus?

There is virtual unanimity among economists of all stripes that the global economic imbalances are unsustainable, and that the U.S. budget deficit in particular must be reduced. Research reports pour out of think tanks, economic research departments, and business lobbying groups urging the United States to cut the budget deficit. A bipartisan coalition of prominent business leaders and former policymakers, including five former Treasury secretaries, has taken out full-page ads in leading newspapers calling for budget balancing. Even popular magazines have run full-length feature articles, such as the one aptly entitled "The Morning After."[1] Doom-and-gloom books occupy top spots on the best-seller lists.[2] The consensus is both domestic and international. A gathering of thirty-three economists from thirteen countries concluded that of the causes of the global imbalances, "the twin deficits of the United States are the largest problem."[3] Where the consensus breaks down is on how to balance the budget and on who is going to take up the resulting slack in the global economy.

The U.S. national debt has almost tripled since 1980, reaching $2.8 trillion in 1988. Budget deficits still loom as far as the eye can see. The United States has moved from being the world's largest creditor to the world's largest debtor, and the debts are still mounting. Some estimate that America's foreign debt could be over $1 trillion by the early 1990s.[4] The U.S. merchandise trade deficit in 1987, $171 billion, was larger than the national income of all but twelve countries, and there is little evidence that it will be eliminated in the near future. The next president will have to take steps to rectify the deficits, and, in doing so, he will have to wrestle with an increasingly hostile Congress.

He will not have much room to maneuver. The interdependence of today's global economy means that the cost of policy mistakes has gone up. And the United States must still live with the consequences of the massive mistake made in 1981 when U.S. fiscal and monetary policy were set upon a collision course, without consideration of the consequences for the world economy. The twin deficits and the financial market turmoil in October 1987 were direct results of that misguided policy.[5]

The next president's task will be all the more difficult if the nation's economy goes into a recession. If a recession does strike, today's difficult problems would be exacerbated. U.S. budget deficits would mushroom, but cutting them would be the wrong medicine. Protectionist pressures would increase. The indebted developing countries could suffer both from reduced industrial country growth and from higher interest rates if the recession were precipitated by a rapid decline in the dollar. And the major industrial countries would engage in a round of mutual recriminations.

Living Beyond Our Means

U.S. national expenditure—the sum of personal consumption, business investment, and government spending—has exceeded gross national product (GNP) in each year since 1981. The excess expenditure is financed by foreign capital inflows that show up as current account deficits in government statistics. The U.S. current account deficit reached $161 billion or 3.6 percent of GNP, in 1987; by contrast, in 1981, the nation registered a $7 billion surplus. After seven successive years of deficits, the United States went from being the world's largest net creditor in 1981, with $140 billion more in assets abroad than in liabilities to foreigners, to having net foreign liabilities of over $400 billion in 1988.

The need to borrow from abroad was caused by large U.S. government budget deficits and low rates of savings by households. The government deficit is a form of dissaving; because households and businesses did not save enough to fund the deficit while simultaneously meeting other investment needs, the difference had to be borrowed from foreigners. This would not have been so serious if the money borrowed from abroad was invested in U.S. productive capacity, but it was not.[6] Instead, it was used to finance consumption.

Investment as a share of GNP between 1982 and 1986 was well below the average for the previous eight years, and business fixed investment continued to decline as foreign borrowing increased. Meanwhile, personal consumption jumped by 2.3 percent of GNP—an amount almost equal to Americans' yearly spending on furniture and household equipment. Only late in 1987, after the stock market crash, did consumption drop off; even then, it rebounded in 1988. At that same time, the personal savings rate as a percentage of after-tax income plummeted to 3.7 percent in 1987, its lowest level in forty years.

America has been on a consumption binge, but such artificial prosperity cannot continue. Just as a household that spends more than it earns by running up credit card debt eventually must spend less than it brings in, sooner or later the United States must service its debt. In other words, Americans will have to produce more than they consume, and sell the difference abroad. Analysts differ on the size of the trade surplus that will be needed to service a trillion-dollar debt to foreigners, but $40 billion to $50 billion is a reasonable estimate.[7] By itself, a trade surplus of this magnitude does not represent a significant hardship for the American people, because it amounts to less than 1 percent of GNP. But adjusting from spending 3.6 percent more than the nation produces to spending 1 percent less than total output will be difficult. If the change happened overnight, Americans would feel as if they had almost 5 percent less to spend each month for food, shelter, and everything else.

This adjustment translates into a swing of roughly $200 billion in the U.S. trade balance. Clearly, this cannot take place in an instant; but it does seem reasonable that it could be done over a period of four to five years, by shifting the trade balance about $40 billion annually.[8] This would require that the growth of national expenditure for personal consumption, business investment, and government spending be held below the growth of output by about one percent annually for the next five years, reversing the pattern of the mid-1980s when the increase in national expenditure in the United States exceeded output growth by about 1 percent. It will also necessitate a shift in national expenditure toward investment and away from consumption.

Can the U.S. trade deficit and dependence upon foreign capital be ended? Only if personal savings can be increased through reduced consumption, if business savings in the form of undistributed corporate profits rise, or if government budget deficits can be reduced. The dissaving by the government in the form of deficits has exceeded the personal savings of individuals for the last five years. Savings rates in the United States have historically been little affected by public policy; Congress cannot markedly change them just by passing a law. That means that in order to free up more goods and services to service foreign-owned debt and to permit more business investment, these hemorrhaging budget deficits must stop.

The federal budget deficit rose from $79 billion, or 2.6 percent of GNP, in 1981 to a peak of $221 billion, or 5.3 percent in 1986. It declined to $150 billion in 1987 as a result of legislative action taken under the Gramm-Rudman-Hollings Budget Act of 1985, which required Congress to pass year-after-year reductions in the deficit or face automatic across-the-board spending cuts. Although this tactic worked initially, its guidelines are now being skirted by the use of optimistic economic forecasts. Future deficits remain above $140 billion.

The necessary adjustment has already begun, but it has a long way to go. The fall of the dollar, which began in 1985, has started to diminish the trade deficit, but the deficit still remains in the range of about $120 billion a year. Export volumes have been increasing at a 20–30 percent annual rate since late 1986, but now capacity restraints threaten to cause a spurt of inflation unless overall spending slows down. Import growth has declined, but imports are still expanding faster than the gross national product. The budget deficit has come down, but it is expected to rise again. The underlying problem of budget deficits and low savings remains.

Budget balancing is essential to restore U.S. credibility abroad. While there is no reason to make balance into a fetish by insisting that each year's expenditures precisely match revenue, large persistent deficits undermine the U.S. economy at home and American prestige abroad. Expenditures must be cut further, but the easy things have all been done. Tax increases cannot be ruled out if the public wants the services the government provides.

The stringent budget constraint ensures that everything depends on everything else. Policymakers will be forced to compare and debate the merits of cutting expenditures for social security or nuclear submarines. Both entitlement and defense expenditures need to be trimmed. Before Congress begins making extreme proposals, however, the next president should preemptively call for a thorough review and justification for all federal programs, including defense. Has the threat to our national security changed or, if not, can the national defense be maintained less expensively? Should entitlement programs be available for all taxpayers, or restricted just to the less well-off? The only way to make sensible choices is to compare the potential savings and consequences of alternative cuts.[9] Without systematic comparisons, poorly developed proposals will emerge from Congress, and that could further undermine U.S. credibility abroad.

Budget Balancing

If the economy is expanding, as it has been since November 1982, budget balancing will certainly be easier. Under those circumstances, the next president should take bold action to reduce the deficit while calling upon the Federal Reserve to accommodate with an easier monetary policy. Indeed, if the economy continues expanding as rapidly as it did in the first-half of 1988, budget cutting or tax increases would be needed to prevent it from overheating.

If the long-awaited recession should hit, the president will not have fiscal policy as a weapon to stimulate demand. Outlays for unemployment insurance will increase and tax revenues will fall; as a result, the deficit will widen. Budget balancing will have to be put off until an expansionary monetary policy leads to a resumption of growth. Monetary policy cannot be eased too rapidly, however, if the dollar is under pressure. In those circumstances, the recession is likely to be protracted.

How much and how fast must the budget deficit be reduced? The reductions should occur gradually so that the risk of a recession is minimized. The aim should be a budget only roughly in balance by 1993, because the deficit can be greatly affected by annual changes in economic conditions. Establishing a trend of declining deficits is the key.

The 1988 budget deficit was approximately $155 billion. With no changes in legislation and assuming a continuation of current economic circumstances, the budget deficit will be $148 billion in 1989 before tapering off by approximately $5 billion annually to $121 billion in 1993, according to the Congressional Budget Office.[10] Outlays in 1988 were 22.3 percent of GNP, while revenues stood at 19.4 percent. If current legislation and economic conditions are assumed to prevail over the next five years, these figures will be little changed in 1993, at 21.9 percent for outlays and 19.4 percent for revenues.[11]

Because they assume no recession and no real growth in military spending, these budget estimates could turn out to be optimistic. Further cuts in defense spending pose a potential problem given the lack of a strategic plan for military spending at a lower level and with designs in the works for a whole host of new military projects. Sam Nunn (D, Ga.), one of the Senate's leading experts on defense spending, has warned of a "bow wave" of future defense spending that, if carried out, could raise defense expenditures over $200 billion above these baseline estimates. To even stay within the range of these estimates, some major weapons systems will have to be scaled back or shelved.[12]

Moreover, all of this assumes no new nondefense spending. The stringent budget constraint leaves little latitude for pursuing new policy initiatives on education, housing, infrastructure, labor adjustment policy, drug abuse prevention and law enforcement, AIDS research, long-term health care, child care, acid rain, or new science projects. Combined, new initiatives in these areas could easily increase federal spending by over $60 billion, or one percent of GNP, in 1993.

Complicating the political debate over the budget is the growing surplus in the social security retirement and disability trust fund. The surplus was approximately $37 billion in 1988. It is expected to rise to $97 billion by 1993, and then rise further into the early years of the next century in order to cover the expected liabilities from the aging of the baby-boom generation.[13]

These surpluses are masking larger deficits in other areas. If the social security surplus is excluded, the federal deficit in 1988 would have been $192 billion, or 3.7 percent of GNP. In 1993, it would be as much as $218 billion, rather than the $121 billion officially estimated. But using the social security surpluses to bankroll current programs will cause budgetary chaos when the trust fund wants to redeem those Treasury notes in order to pay retirement benefits some twenty-five years hence. If the integrity of the surpluses is to be maintained, the amount of deficit reduction needed is greater, on the order of $200 billion to $220 billion or approaching 4 percent of GNP in 1993. From a macroeconomic standpoint, however, the overall budget deficit taking the social security surplus into account is the appropriate aggregate to focus upon. And from there, a less-ambitious goal would be a reduction of the 1993 deficit by $120 billion to $125 billion provided that no new major spending initiatives are launched in the nondefense area. If this lower target is selected, baby-boomers had better start saving more for their retirement now because the social security trust fund will not be sufficient to cover all beneficiaries. Benefits for future retirees will probably have to be reduced.

Consider the following budget basics. Broken down into its component parts, 28 percent of the budget goes for defense; 47 percent is committed to mandatory expenditures, mostly for entitlements (social security and medicare), and approximately 14 percent is for interest on the outstanding government debt. That leaves only about 11 to 12 percent for all other nondefense, discretionary expenditures. In other words, if defense and entitlement spending remain unchanged and debt is serviced, over 90 percent of all other government programs and personnel would have to be eliminated in order to balance the budget in 1989. That is impossible. Little savings can be expected from these programs, particularly since a bipartisan consensus has emerged in Congress over the past several years that these are the programs that constituents want.[14]

That, therefore, leaves defense, mandatory programs, and interest on the debt. Interest on the national debt cannot be avoided, although if interest rates were to fall, its magnitude would be reduced. Inflation-adjusted interest rates are high because of the continuing need to attract foreign capital. If a credible, multiyear legislative package ensuring declining deficits were put into place, interest rates would then decline.[15] Even a one-point drop in interest rates would yield substantial annual budget savings now that the federal debt is approaching $3 trillion.

The two most politically sensitive expenditures, defense and entitlement spending, remain as sources of potential budget cuts. One of the daunting challenges of reducing both types of spending is that major changes in these programs require a restructuring of an entire array of policies. The objective should be to slow the growth in defense and entitlement expenditures over the next several years. The critical political ingredient will be to develop a balanced package in which the pain is shared equitably across the American public.

Some tough choices lie ahead. Several options for cutting expenditures under consideration by the Congressional Budget

Table 1

Budget Deficit Reduction Options on the Expenditure Side
(*Annual Savings in $ billions*)

Option	Fiscal year 1990	Fiscal year 1993
Freeze defense spending at 1988 levels until 1993	$19.0	$58.0
Freeze nondefense discretionary spending at 1988 levels until 1993	7.0	24.0
Impose a one-year freeze on all programs in 1989	31.0	46.0
Impose a one-year freeze on defense programs and pay	9.0	12.0
Establish a means test for medicare*	10.0	30.0
Reduce cost-of-living adjustment on non-means-tested programs by 2 percent for 5 years	10.0	29.0
End the Economic Development Administration, Urban Development Action Grants, Community Development Block Grants and Legal Services Corporation	4.0	4.0
Reduce foreign assistance by 25 percent*	4.0	4.0
Cut federal workforce by 50,000	0.2	1.0

Source: Congressional Budget Office, *Reducing the Deficit: Spending and Revenue Options* (Washington, D.C.: U.S. Government Printing Office, March 1988).

* These estimates were provided by Richard Brandon and reported in "Budget Discussion Paper" (Working Paper for a Council on Foreign Relations study group on the Economic Choices Confronting the Next President, New York, June 7, 1988).

Office are shown in Table 1, offering a rough estimate of the effect of each change upon the budget.

Even the extreme step of freezing defense and nondefense discretionary programs at 1988 levels for five years would reduce annual expenditures by only $82 billion in 1993, leaving a deficit of roughly $40 billion. No one is seriously proposing such an extended freeze because it would wreak havoc on U.S. programs and policies. A one-year freeze in 1989 covering all programs would reduce the budget deficit by $46 billion in 1993, yet it would leave the new president with no flexibility to offer new programs of his own during his critical first year in office. A one-year freeze of defense spending alone in 1989 would lower expenditures by only $12 billion in 1993.

Defense cuts will attract particular attention in the wake of the Pentagon spending and procurement scandals revealed in the summer of 1988. Defense expenditures expanded rapidly during the Reagan administration. Even though inflation-adjusted defense expenditures declined by 6 percent between 1985 and 1988, the $291 billion budgeted for 1988 was still $30 billion above the total that would have been expected if three percent annual real growth had occurred between 1980 and 1988. Most defense cuts, unfortunately, do not yield much short-term savings, because the commitments to procure weapons systems are spread over a period of years, covering research, development, testing, and, ultimately, production. Furthermore, over 50 percent of defense spending is allocated to personnel; it is difficult to trim personnel and to delay pay raises. Even cutting defense expenditures by $35 billion from the forecasts (about 0.5 percent of GNP in 1993) will require rearranging force structures and may also pose strains for military and political alliances. But the forecasts assume only small increases in defense spending to keep up with inflation. They do not address the commitments made but not budgeted for in the Reagan defense buildup, including the Strategic Defense Initiative and a 600-ship navy. A major review and reassessment of military affairs and objectives is overdue.

Several options for cutting nondefense spending are also set out in Table 1. The most significant reductions are possible in entitlement programs. The biggest item could also be the most controversial. If medicare benefits were available only to individuals under a certain income level, up to $30 billion would be saved in 1993.[16] A means test would have to be established in order to determine eligibility. But this would have to be done through the tax system, because only on tax forms does the government learn how much total income taxpayers receive.

When the benefits are recaptured from well-off taxpayers, they are likely to complain that their taxes are being raised.

Reducing the cost-of-living adjustment in social security and all other non-means-tested programs is commonly proposed as an effective way to slow the growth in entitlement spending. Social security, and veterans and government pension benefits are now adjusted annually to offset the increase in the consumer price index. If the cost-of-living adjustment were set two percent below the consumer price index for five years, expenditures would be reduced by $29 billion in 1993. Since the majority of the recipients are already retired, however, a five-year cut in cost-of-living adjustments would threaten their standard of living.

Beyond the entitlement programs, other nondefense cuts yield little savings and can be made only with some sacrifice of national objectives. For instance, in foreign assistance, a 25 percent reduction would cut expenditures by $4 billion in 1993, but at considerable cost to overseas objectives and operations. Elimination of the Economic Development Administration, various block grants, and the Legal Services Corporation combined yields only $4 billion in 1993. And cutting the federal work force by 50,000 employees or 2 percent, a popular proposal, reduces expenditures by only $1 billion in 1993.

Agricultural programs, which along with defense were among the few programs to expand under the Reagan administration, are estimated to cost $18 to $19 billion annually from 1988 to 1993, but because of the vagaries of weather and changes in world market conditions, outlays could fluctuate considerably. Expenditures on agricultural programs reached a record of $26 billion in 1986. While small amounts of restraint could be included as part of a budget reduction package, the political pain inflicted by reducing agricultural programs significantly would probably prevent that from occurring. Furthermore, agricultural subsidies are currently under multilateral negotiation, and agricultural interest groups will argue that any cut in U.S. price supports should be contingent upon subsidy reduction by other countries.

If cutting expenditures proves insufficient, as seems likely, then revenues will have to be raised. Leaving aside payroll taxes,

Table 2

Budget Deficit Reduction Options on the Revenue Side
(*Annual Gains in $ billions*)

Option	Fiscal year 1990	Fiscal year 1993
Change Rates		
Establish a 33 percent tax bracket for households with income over $200,000	$6.0	$8.0
Raise marginal tax rates to 16 percent and 30 percent	28.0	36.0
Repeal indexing	12.0	52.0
Delay indexing until 1990	6.0	8.0
Broaden Base		
Limit mortgage interest deduction to 15 percent tax bracket	11.0	15.0
Eliminate deductability of state and local taxes	26.0	32.0
Excise Taxes		
Impose a 5 percent value-added or national sales tax with exemptions for food, housing, and medical care	44.0	80.0
Impose a $5 tax on domestic and imported oil	21.0	22.0
Increase gasoline taxes 12 cents per gallon	11.0	12.0
Raise cigarette tax to 32 cents per pack (from 16 cents)	3.0	3.0
Raise taxes on beer and wine to rate on distilled spirits	4.0	4.0

Source: Congressional Budget Office, *Reducing the Deficit: Spending and Revenue Options* (Washington, D.C.: U.S. Government Printing Office, March 1988).

which are currently used for social security, revenues can be raised from three sources: higher rates on personal or corporate taxes; a broadening of the tax base; and higher excise taxes. A menu of various revenue options is included in Table 2.

Even substantial changes in the tax code do not yield revenues sufficient to halve the deficit in 1993. Establishing a 33 percent top tax bracket, rather than the current 28 percent, for households earning over $200,000 would raise only an additional $8 billion in 1993. Raising marginal tax rates to 16 percent and 30 percent (from 15 percent and 28 percent) would generate $36 billion in new revenue. An increase in the top marginal rate for corporations from 34 percent to 35 percent would generate only $3 billion per year in 1993. Base broadening would help, but eliminating the deduction for state and local taxes and restricting mortgage interest deductions to the lower 15 percent bracket would raise only $47 billion in 1993. Increased excise taxes—including a 12-cent gasoline tax and higher "sin" taxes on cigarettes, beer, and wine—would yield $19 billion in 1993. On the other hand, a 5 percent value-added tax, with exceptions for food, housing, and medical expenses, would yield $80 billion in 1993.

Clearly, if the budget cannot come close to being balanced by reducing outlays, then one of the major revenue options will have to be selected. Each of these options, however, is politically contentious. Many liberals oppose a value-added tax because it might end up falling disproportionately on the poor; and many conservatives are against it because it would be too easy to ratchet the rate upward. Some revenue options, like repealing the deduction for state and local taxes, were major battlegrounds in the fight over the 1986 tax act and would surely become so again; Congress will be reluctant to rewrite the tax code so soon after the 1986 reform. Doing away with the indexation of rates and deductions for inflation is by far the largest untapped source of expanding revenue—it would generate an additional $52 billion in 1993—but many legislators advocate indexing for the discipline it provides over spending.

If the president wants to avoid a negative reaction from the financial markets, which would plunge the United States into recession, he should consider the following package to roughly balance the budget of 1993. Reductions should start with a one-year freeze on defense, while a comprehensive review of military missions and strategies is conducted. This would yield $12 billion in 1993. If further savings can be obtained in weapons systems or personnel, perhaps defense expenditures could be reduced by as much as $35 billion in 1993. Eliminating medicare for the well-off would yield $30 billion. Assuming another $5 billion could be cut from other programs and figuring on a one percentage point drop in interest rates ($30 billion), total expenditures could be reduced by $100 billion in 1993. But this is still below even the less ambitious deficit reduction target of $120 billion to $125 billion. Tax increases in the $20 billion to $30 billion range will be needed. These cuts could be painful for the body politic, however, and could come at some sacrifice to our national defense. If they prove too painful or too risky, the tax increases will have to be higher.

On the revenue side, delaying indexing for two years would yield $8 billion in 1993. A 33 percent bracket for very well-off taxpayers would produce $8 billion, and would undoubtedly play a catalytic role in selling the package to the American people. Increased excise taxes would be consistent with a shift away from consumption and could be phased in over time. A twenty-cent gasoline tax would bring in approximately $20 billion, and higher "sin" taxes on beer, wine, and cigarettes would supply $7 billion. That adds up to $43 billion in additional revenues. And if monetary policy were eased and growth were to accelerate, even more revenue could be generated. Should high deficits continue to be a problem, however, further tax increases will be required. Indexing could be postponed further, perhaps through 1993, and this delay would produce $44 billion in additional revenue. Alternatively, the marginal rates could be increased to 16 percent and 30 percent, to yield $36 billion more revenue in 1993. If defense and entitlements cannot be slashed, one of these two revenue options should be used to balance the budget in 1993 under the less-ambitious goal of a $120–$125 billion reduction. Much larger tax increases on the order of $90 billion to $100 billion more would be necessary if the integrity of the social security surpluses is to be preserved.

Whatever course he chooses to balance the budget, it is critical that the next president act decisively to develop the package early on and in close consultation with Congress. If budget deficits can be set upon a declining path, the growth of debt can be slowed, the cost of investment can be lowered, and credibility can be established at home and abroad. Having embarked on this difficult road, the president can then turn to the steps that may need to be taken in concert with other countries on both military and economic affairs.

Burden-Bearing or Burden-Sharing?

With the stringent budget constraint leaving little latitude for pursuing new policy initiatives and making it necessary to trim old programs or increase taxes, Congress is asking the allies to bear more of the burden for the common defense. Proposals appear from time to time, but they are gaining more adherents from across the political spectrum, both because balancing the budget has been so difficult and because the other industrial countries have successfully rebuilt and now are in a position to afford more. If deep defense cuts are necessary, members of Congress are likely to recommend cutting down on troops and materials overseas rather than curtailing production of weapons in their own districts. There is little constituency for troops stationed abroad; the soldiers can vote, but most would not vote to remain abroad. The problem is that not that much money can be saved by pulling U.S. troops out of Europe or the Pacific, unless they are demobilized, because they must eat and be paid wherever they are.

The increased demand for burden-sharing is fueled by several key comparisons. In 1986, the United States spent 6.7 percent of national income on defense compared with an average of 3.5 percent for the other countries that belong to the North Atlantic Treaty Organization (NATO). Japan, not in NATO, is constitutionally limited to spending only 1 percent of its national income on defense. U.S. defense outlays on a per-capita basis amounted to $1,155 in 1986, compared with $318 for other NATO countries and $163 for Japan. Table 3 compares contributions relative to the ability to contribute.

With 48 percent of the combined national income, the United States contributes 70 percent of NATO defense spending. On manpower and naval tonnage, U.S. contributions also exceed the country's population and national income shares. However, on

Table 3

Burden-Sharing (1985)

Indicators of Ability to Contribute to the Western Defense*

Contributor	National income (as % of total)	Population (as % of total)	Per-capita national Income (% of U.S. level)
United States	48%	32%	100%
Other NATO members	36	53	45
Japan	17	16	70

Contributions to the Western Defense (% of total)*

Contributor	Defense spending	Total defense manpower	Ground forces	Tactical air force	Naval tonnage
United States	70%	38%	39%	45%	64%
Other NATO members	27	59	57	51	33
Japan	4	2	4	4	3

Ratios: Contributions/Ability to Contribute

Contributor	Defense spending/ national income	Defense manpower/ population	Ground forces/ national income	Tactical air forces/ national income	Naval tonnage/ national income
United States	1.47	1.22	0.82	0.96	1.35
Other NATO members	0.74	1.13	1.61	1.42	0.92
Japan	0.21	0.14	0.22	0.23	0.19

Source: Richard Brandon, "Budget Discussion Paper" (Working Paper for a Council on Foreign Relations study group on the Economic Choices Confronting the Next President, New York, June 7, 1988), p. 14.

* If figures do not add up to 100 percent, it is because of rounding.

ground and tactical air forces, other NATO countries chip in far more than the United States; they provide 57 percent of the ground forces and 51 percent of the tactical forces, compared with 41 percent and 45 percent, respectively, by the United States. Except for Japan, which contributes far less than both the United States and other NATO countries in all categories, it is not clear which countries contribute more to the alliance defense. It depends which yardstick is being used as a measure.

Being a leader is expensive. Great powers have great interests and great responsibilities. American demands for increased burden-sharing alienate allies and make it even more difficult to find solutions. Furthermore, if the United States did reduce its contributions, it is not clear that the allies would take up all the slack. Some in Europe might use the opportunity to adopt a more accommodating policy towards the Soviet Union. If the allies do agree to provide relatively more to the common defense, however, they will inevitably want to have more of a voice in deciding how resources are deployed and how and when to intervene with force.

What, then, can be done? For one thing, the United States could ask the NATO allies to work together to eliminate the "interoperability problem" in Europe. Currently the allies are buying six different types of battle tanks, six different fighter aircraft, and units in the field cannot even communicate with each other because of the utilization of six different communications systems.[17]

Rationalization and standardization are long overdue. Although some U.S. and European manufacturers would undoubtedly complain, as they have in the past to derail efforts to integrate defense capabilities, it surely would improve the alliance's military preparedness.[18] With the European Community engaged in an effort to create a Europe without borders by 1992, and with the revival of defense cooperation in the Western European Union, the prospects for rationalization and standardization appear better now than ever. In order to modernize and improve the alliance's conventional forces in the wake of the agreement covering intermediate nuclear forces, the next president should welcome European initiatives for establishing a common market in defense goods. Rather than finger pointing and bean counting, the allies should be talking about shared interests and shared responsibilities, and should move away from the more emotive term, "burden-sharing."

The next president must have a clear understanding of the strategic importance of our relationships with and initiatives toward other countries. He should tread very carefully before replacing burden-bearing with burden-sharing. Former President Nixon made a sound proposal when he suggested that the next president's first summit should be with NATO allies, not with Soviet leader Mikhail Gorbachev.[19] By spending time with them discussing common interests and joint responsibilities, the president could signal U.S. leadership and reliability while urging them to do more to provide for the defense of the alliance. Such a meeting would also serve as a useful signal to Congress that he is giving serious attention to alliance commitments.

The burden-sharing issue could also command attention if the next president surrenders to the temptation to use U.S. security clout in order to obtain economic objectives. Although security and economic issues will undoubtedly compete as priorities for the president's attention when he meets with foreign leaders, he should avoid deliberately linking the two in pressing foreign governments to act. Since World War II, the United States has attempted to compartmentalize security and economic affairs in the conduct of foreign policy, and, by and large, that effort has served well.[20] Linkage would be a recipe for inconsistency and incoherence and would alter the political contours of U.S. alliances. It could vastly complicate matters and ensure a paralysis of policymaking, particularly since each area is dominated by a separate set of experts. Both security and economic affairs are complicated enough on their own, and a stubborn stalemate on economic policy already exists.

Getting Other Countries to Act

Budget deficit reduction should be the first priority of the next administration, but not all of the world's economic problems can be laid at America's doorstep. America's trade balances are also dependent on the economic growth of its major trading partners. Since the global recession of 1982–83, growth in Europe has been weak, exacerbating the U.S. trade deficit. Similarly, as some developing countries have struggled to service their debts, they have been unable to afford to buy U.S. exports, another factor adding to the trade deficit. Latin America, once a major market for U.S. products, has been devastated.

The decline of the dollar and the eventual elimination of the budget deficit will mean that the United States will purchase less from the rest of the world, and someone else will have to pick up the slack. Just as growth in domestic expenditures in the United States exceeded that of output from 1982 to 1987, with the world economy benefiting from the additional sales to American buyers, now other economies will have to step up expenditure growth faster than output growth and buy more overseas to do their share in sustaining the health of the international economy.

Which countries are going to take reduced trade surpluses or bigger deficits? It is unlikely to be the developing countries, many of which are already fighting to service their debts. The developing countries as a whole had a combined current account deficit of $20 billion in 1987, although Taiwan and South Korea do enjoy large surpluses. Therefore, the major adjustment will have to be among the industrial countries. The twenty-one industrial countries that are members of the Organization for Economic Cooperation and Development other than the United States, Germany and Japan had a combined current account deficit in 1987 of about $20 billion. If the U.S. current account deficit is going to be reduced, it follows that most of the improvement would probably be reflected in sharp decreases in the surpluses of Germany ($44 billion) and Japan ($87 billion).[12] These two nations must expand their domestic economies and liberalize their markets, otherwise the world economy could slip into a recession. Further currency appreciation by these countries may also be required as it will be for Taiwan and South Korea.

What initiatives can the president take to get the surplus countries to do their part? Three options are available. The United States could make its internal adjustments and let markets work their will; it could take a shock-therapy action like imposing an import surcharge; or it could continue present efforts at coordination while increasing economic pressure.

The first option would be a hand's off approach relying on market forces to change other countries' policies.[22] Rather than negotiating with other countries to work out an elaborate coordinated package of macroeconomic measures, the next president could let it be known publicly that the United States would no longer waste its efforts in such a manner. The dollar would then decline, which would put pressure on the surplus countries to act in order to prevent their declining exports from inducing a recession. One sure way to get other countries to respond is if they see that it is in their own interest to do so.

Efforts at cooperation are very time-consuming. If agreement cannot be reached on the actions to be taken when economic circumstances change, they are bound to fail and that will unsettle markets. Furthermore, since U.S. exports and growth are affected little by growth in other countries, why bother urging them to grow? The problem with this option is that timing is everything. A decline in the dollar and the eventual elimination of the U.S. budget deficit will have a contractionary effect worldwide comparable to that of the second oil shock in 1979.[23] If other countries do not expand domestic demand faster to compensate for the contraction, a recession could result. In addition, the industrial economies are linked not only through trade in goods but through financial channels. Relying on markets alone could lead the dollar to collapse, thereby unsettling financial markets. Interest rates would rise and a full-blown worldwide recession would ensue.

Advocates of a shock-therapy approach claim a crisis is needed in order to concentrate minds and to force action. One way to start a crisis would be to drive the dollar down, but that would send the world economy into a recession. An alternative is to impose an import surcharge. The Trade Act of 1974 authorizes the president to impose an import surcharge of up to 15 percent for one hundred fifty days, at which time it must come off unless Congress acts to extend it. The primary motive, of course, would be to get the attention of the surplus countries and to increase U.S. leverage in getting them to act. If they stimulate their economies sufficiently, the import surcharge could then be lifted. Imposition of a surcharge would also serve as a signal to Congress that the president seriously wants action from the surplus countries. And it would raise revenue. As part of a package, an import surcharge would help push the Congress into being more forthcoming. But most of this could also be accomplished by just threatening to impose a surcharge, and there are significant drawbacks, which should be recognized.

The Nixon surcharge in August 1971 got international attention, but the world is much different today. Production around the world is much more integrated. A surcharge would penalize domestic producers that rely upon imported parts and components. Under today's flexible exchange rates with large volumes of highly mobile, interest-sensitive funds, imposition of a surcharge could cause a run on the dollar.

A surcharge would also focus too much attention on the foreign component of the macroeconomic imbalances, diverting attention from the necessary domestic action. If the surcharge were imposed, Congress might find it a ready source of revenue and want to extend it. By reinforcing the view that the United States is shirking the mantle of leadership, it would also not be the most conducive way to forge new relationships with other countries. Starting an economic shooting war so early in a new administration would be dangerous, particularly since other countries have the ability to wreak havoc by suggesting that investors take their money out of the United States. Foreign countries could also retaliate with surcharges of their own.

The third option would be to continue present efforts at coordination but with added pressure applied. The first step would be the development of a multiyear budget reduction package with sustainable expenditure cuts and tax increases. Such a package would restore U.S. credibility and leverage with other countries. After getting Congress to agree to the package, the president could telephone leaders of other major industrial countries, in particular Germany and Japan, before the legislation is signed. He could tell them that the United States is prepared to own up to its part of the bargain and inquire what actions they are prepared to take. Other countries should be urged to step up domestic demand and to cooperate in holding the dollar down. (The Federal Reserve could help in this effort by easing monetary policy.) His key economic advisors could be dispatched to a meeting of finance ministers and central bankers of the summit countries, and they could be directed to put together a multicountry package of economic reforms for announcement at the economic summit in July 1989. If the president wants to maximize his leverage, he could refuse to sign the legislation until they agreed to act, but such a game of macroeconomic "chicken" would harm the prospects for long-term cooperation. And the budget balancing ought to be done in the U.S. interest, whether or not the other major industrial countries are prepared to go along. If they refuse to go along, market forces through falling exports and sluggish growth would eventually prod them into action. He should forcefully remind them that they too have a responsibility to manage interdependence, particularly since their economies remain much more dependent upon developments in the rest of the world economy than does the United States. This should be the preferred option.

Above all, the next president should remember the "first law of holes"—when you are in one, stop digging![24] The sooner U.S. budget deficits are brought under control, the smaller the debt service requirements will be in the future, and the sooner America will again project an image as the world's economic leader.

Notes

1. Peter G. Peterson, "The Morning After," *The Atlantic Monthly*, October 1987, pp. 43–69.
2. Ravi Batra's *The Great Depression of 1990: Why It's Got to Happen* (New York: Simon and Schuster, 1987) was on the *New York Times* best-seller list for thirty-eight weeks in 1987–88. As of August 21, 1988, Paul Kennedy's widely discussed book, *The Rise and Fall of the Great Powers* (New York: Random House, 1988) was on the list for twenty-nine weeks. Kennedy's book was focused not solely on economics but on the balance between resources and defense commitments. Kennedy warned of "imperial overstretch" and his arguments are being widely touted by those who would have the United States do less overseas while calling upon allies to share more of the defense burden.
3. *Resolving the Global Economic Crisis: After Wall Street, A Statement by 33 Economists from 13 Countries* (Washington, D.C.: Institute for International Economics, 1987), p. 16. Similarly, both the International Monetary Fund and the Organization for Economic Cooperation and Development have called, and repeatedly so, for U.S. budget deficit reduction.
4. Morgan Guaranty, "Global Growth and Adjustment at Risk," *World Financial Markets* (September/October 1987), p. 4, and David Hale, "Risks to Foreign Investors in the U.S.," *The International Economy*, vol. II, no. 3 (May/June 1988), p. 9.

5. For an extended discussion of the relationship between the trade and budget deficits and the causes of the dollar appreciation, see Shafiqul Islam, "The Dollar and the Policy-Performance-Confidence Mix," *Princeton Essays in International Finance*, no. 170 (July 1988).

6. While U.S. foreign borrowing rose by 3.5 percent of GNP between 1982 and 1986, the federal budget deficit rose by almost 3 percent and personal savings declined by 1.5 percent, compared with the period 1973–81. America began to borrow heavily from abroad in 1982 at the same time that gross private investment reached a trough. For the period 1982–86, gross private investment as a share of GNP was one percent lower than in 1973–81 period, and business fixed investment continued to decline as foreign borrowing increased. Shafiqul Islam, "America's Foreign Debt: Fear, Fantasy, Fiction & Facts" (Paper presented at the Congressional Research Service Workshop, Washington, D.C., April 1, 1988, mimeographed).

7. This is lower than a simple calculation of applying a 7 percent or 8 percent interest rate to a trillion dollars because of the difference in the rate of return on U.S. assets and liabilities, the prospects that the United States will earn growing surpluses on services trade, and the likelihood that some of the debt servicing will occur through asset sales. For a detailed analysis, see Islam, "America's Foreign Debt," *op. cit.*

8. Steven Marris, *Deficits and the Dollar Revisited* (Washington, D.C.: Institute for International Economics, 1987), pp. 13–18.

9. One opportunity for a dispassionate, thorough-going review of government policies and programs, and the adequacy of the revenue base needed to support those programs, is provided by the bipartisan National Economic Commission established in 1987. It is chaired by Robert Strauss, U.S. trade representative under President Carter, and Drew Lewis, secretary of transportation under President Reagan. The commission consists of twelve members, six from each party and the next president can appoint two members after the election. The commission's recommendations are due March 31, 1989. The hope is that this commission will, like the Greenspan Commission that made the recommendations for revamping social security in 1983, provide political cover so that politicians and the new president can make the tough choices with minimal domestic outcry. The commission may also make recommendations on budget reform. One reform that deserves consideration is a two-year budgetary cycle. Congress now spends most of its effort with the various budget and authorization bills, leaving it precious little time to spend debating other policy issues. The result is that many pieces of legislation are rolled into large omnibus bills that often do not get the close scrutiny that they deserve. A two-year budget cycle would help to alleviate the situation.

10. Congressional Budget Office, *Reducing the Deficit: Spending and Revenue Options* (Washington, D.C.: U.S. Government Printing Office, March 1988) and revised estimates in The Economic and Budget Outlook: An Update (August 1988). The budget numbers are for the fiscal year which runs from October 1 of the previous year to September 30 of the listed year.

11. Congressional Budget Office, *The Economic and Budget Outlook: Fiscal Years 1989–1993* (Washington, D.C.: U.S. Government Printing Office, 1988).

12. Leonard Silk, "The New Guns-and-Butter Battle," *New York Times*, May 22, 1988, sect. 3, p. 1.

13. The political problem is that these surpluses look like a ready source of funds for financing new programs. Confirming this suspicion, opinion articles have already started to appear suggesting possible uses for the funds. See, for example, W.W. Rostow, "For a Public Investment Bank," *New York Times*, July 7, 1988; the author argued "I propose that the surplus be used as a basis for a Public Investment Bank." p. A23. Also see George E. Brown, Jr., "Invest Social Security Surplus," *Journal of Commerce*, November 24, 1987, p. 10A.

14. David A. Stockman, *The Triumph of Politics: Why the Reagan Revolution Failed* (New York: Harper and Row, 1986), pp. 376–77.

15. See Martin S. Feldstein, "Halving the Pain of Budget Balance," *Wall Street Journal*, May 25, 1988, p. 24.

16. Richard Brandon, "Budget Discussion Paper" (Working Paper for a Council on Foreign Relations study group on the Economic Choices Confronting the Next President, New York, June 7, 1988, mimeographed).

17. Richard F. Kaufman, "The Global Shakedown," *The International Economy*, vol. II, no. 3 (May/June 1988), pp. 118–22.

18. Ibid.

19. Richard M. Nixon, *1999: Victory Without War* (New York: Simon and Schuster, 1988), p. 207. A similar admonition was made by David Calleo, Harold van B. Cleveland, and Leonard Silk in "The Dollar and the Defense of the West," *Foreign Affairs*, vol. 66, no. 1 (Spring 1988), where they said "it is imperative that the United States not become so preoccupied with Soviet relations that it fails to make the fundamental changes in the West that are the precondition for future stability within the global system." p. 862.

20. Gregory F. Treverton, in chapter 5 of *Making the Alliance Work: The United States and Western Europe* (London and Ithaca, N.Y.: Macmillan and Cornell University Press, 1985) concludes that on balance the separation has served the alliance well.

21. Robert Solomon, "The United States as an International Debtor," *International Economic Letter*, vol. VII, no. 4 (April 16, 1988), p. 6.

22. Martin S. Feldstein, "The End of Policy Coordination," *Wall Street Journal*, November 9, 1987, p. 26. He argues that "a doubling of current real gross national product growth rates in Europe and Japan would raise U.S. exports by only $5 billion and U.S. gross national product by only 1 percent." But since the U.S. trade deficit is larger than the GNP of all but twelve countries, a closing of that gap will surely be felt elsewhere.

23. Morgan Guaranty, "Reducing the Twin Deficits," *World Financial Markets*, no. 2 (May 1988), p. 13.
24. Robert D. Hormats brought this pithy aphorism to our attention.

3

Managing the World's Money

The link between America's imbalance of savings and investment and the world economy can be found flickering on computer screens in corporate treasurers' offices and banks' trading rooms around the world. There, constantly changing price quotations reveal the action in the global currency market. Unlike the markets for stocks, bonds, wheat futures, and Treasury bills, the currency market has no central trading floor, no organization, no regulations. Face-to-face dealings are the exception, telephone or computer transactions the rule. The volume of purchases and sales can only be guessed at. Yet, this ill-defined and unmanaged electronic market, which determines the relative values of the world's major trading currencies, has a critical role in shaping international patterns of production and trade.

This has been the case to an ever greater extent since August 15, 1971, when President Richard Nixon revoked the U.S. government's long-standing pledge to convert the dollar holdings of foreign countries into gold at the rate of $35 an ounce, marking the end of the system of fixed exchange rates that the United States and forty-three other nations established at Bretton Woods, New Hampshire, in 1944. Subsequently, the economies of the United States and its trading partners have experienced enormous economic turbulence as the currency markets, by and large, have been allowed to determine the relative values of different countries' monies. During Ronald Reagan's presidency, the value of the dollar against other major currencies rose to remarkable heights between 1981 and 1985, and then fell from its peak by more than half during the ensuing two years. President Reagan's successor will face strong pressure to find a way to bring such massive fluctuations under control.

Stabilizing exchange rates is not a particularly difficult task. Economists of diverse opinions have circulated dozens of different, well-conceived proposals that would accomplish it. If the Federal Reserve Board is willing to raise or lower interest rates as required, almost any of the programs would work. Each of the proposals, however, has a cost in terms of the sacrifice of other economic objectives. The question confronting the president, then, is essentially one that requires a value judgment: given his broader goals for the United States, how much importance should be accorded the stabilization of the dollar's rate of foreign exchange?

By and large, the question of exchange rate stability has received far too much attention in discussions of the nation's economic problems. The value of the dollar is not and should not be the U.S. government's principal economic concern.

How Much Do Exchange Rates Matter?

At first glance, the issue seems of paramount importance. The volume of trading in foreign exchange is enormous, swamping the flows of goods, services, and international investment. By 1986, more than $330 billion was changing hands in foreign exchange markets daily, compared with an average of $5.8 billion in trade on a daily basis.

With the increasing volume of international trade and the large flows of cross-border investment, exchange rates have become an important influence on economic performance. Much of the growth in the U.S. trade deficit during the 1980s can be traced to the relatively high international value of the dollar from 1981 to 1987. According to one estimate, every 1 percent increase in the value of the dollar during that period (measured against a basket of currencies according to their importance in

U.S. trade) led to a 0.16 percent fall in manufacturing employment, with even stronger effects in durable goods industries such as automobiles and electric machinery. Between 1980 and 1985, the change in the dollar's value is estimated to have reduced manufacturing employment by 1.1 million jobs.[1] Exchange rates that fluctuate far from their average long-term levels, as the dollar has for most of this decade, can have serious economic effects, including wide variations in consumption from one year to the next, alternating deflationary and inflationary pressures, and the consequences of closing down industries and laying off workers as imports suddenly gain a price advantage.[2]

Prolonged misalignment of exchange rates also distorts the relative prices of products that are traded internationally against those that are not. The result is unsound investment decisions. If country A's currency rises sharply against country B's, citizens of country A will find tradable goods so cheap as compared with nontradables that they will likely underinvest in production of machinery and consumer products while putting too much capital into beauty salons and restaurants, which face no import competition. Country B's citizens, conversely, will overinvest in tradables. In both countries, this investment pattern, distorted by unsustainable currency fluctuations, results in inefficient use of capital and unwise career decisions by workers who may presume that relative prices in the future will remain as they are at present.

The impact of currency trading on the world economy, however, is far smaller than the large volume of transactions would suggest. Over 85 percent of the currency dealing during 1986 occurred either among banks or between banks and other financial organizations, all of which held very short-term positions in the spot market in order to earn trading profits. In many of these cases, traders were in and out of the market in a matter of hours. Only a tiny proportion of foreign exchange activity involved other types of businesses, such as manufacturers. Although some companies do make use of the currency futures markets in order to hedge their business risks, currency futures trading accounted for only one-twentieth of the foreign exchange transactions undertaken by banks.[3]

As the international value of a country's currency rises and falls, only a portion of the change gets passed along to consumers and businesses in the form of higher or lower prices. In the United States, import prices fell far less between 1980 and 1985 than the 56 percent rise in the trade-weighted value of the dollar would have predicted. The reason may have been that foreign firms, convinced that they would face extremely favorable exchange rates only temporarily, chose to maintain high prices and high profit margins rather than cutting prices in order to gain market share.[4] Conversely, as the dollar fell from its high point of February 1985, import prices responded only sluggishly.[5] The prices of Japan's exports to the United States rose far more slowly, in dollar terms, than the costs of Japanese producers, while the U.S. price of Swedish-built Volvos rose only 17 percent over a period when Swedish labor costs were increasing by 70 percent, expressed in dollars.[6] One careful study of a key Canadian export in the U.S. market revealed that the fall of the Canadian dollar against the U.S. dollar from 1975 to 1985 had only minor effects on prices.[7]

Day-to-day exchange rate volatility probably has some impact on international trade, as producers and their customers attempt to reduce their uncertainty by minimizing their dependence on exports and imports from countries with unstable currencies. But that effect hardly qualifies short-term volatility as a major economic problem. When major currencies are involved, businesses expecting to undertake a transaction at a specific date in the near future can use futures markets to lock in an exchange rate, minimizing their exposure to volatility even more. The threat that exchange rates may suddenly be quite different tomorrow may discourage some U.S. companies from exporting, but it is far less important than economic conditions at home and abroad in determining the volume of trade.[8]

Clearly, less exchange rate fluctuation would bring economic benefits. Those benefits, however, should not be overstated. Any effort to reform the international monetary system must take into account the fact that, despite their shortcomings, flexible exchange rates continue to mark an improvement over the perennially crisis-plagued fixed rate system that preceded them, a system that was unable to adapt to changes in countries' relative economic health. And, limiting exchange rate flexibility may impose costs on the U.S. economy that are even more unattractive than an overvalued dollar, such as a lessened ability to use monetary policy to control inflation or to permit economic expansion.

When the industrial countries moved from a fixed to a floating rate system in the early 1970s, one of the hopes was that floating rates would put an end to the economic crises that arose under fixed rates every time one country's exchange rate got out of line. Under the fixed rate system, if the country was unwilling to adjust its economic policies to keep the exchange rate stable, then speculators' bets that the rate would change forced central banks to pour out massive sums of money to purchase German marks or French francs or British pounds in order to hold up their price until, eventually, finance ministers held an urgent meeting and decreed new exchange rates for the currency concerned. Under a floating rate system, by contrast, if countries choose to pursue divergent economic policies, no exchange rate crisis would ensue; instead, exchange rates would adjust gradually, on a daily basis, to the policies in each country.

Similarly, proponents of floating rates hoped, if one country proved to have a chronic trade deficit under floating rates, the relatively low demand for its currency and its citizens' relatively high demand for foreign money would cause the exchange rate to adjust automatically until trade came back into balance. Floating rates would put an end to the need for large and sudden exchange rate changes, such as the 17 percent devaluation of the pound in December 1967, since smaller changes could occur from day to day.[9]

Although it has been far from perfect, the floating rate system has worked well compared to the systems that preceded it. During its first years, exchange rate movements were relatively smooth (if each country's rate is measured against a basket of other currencies), and currency futures markets expanded quickly to allow businesses to hedge against the risk of exchange rate change. In the past decade, problems have occurred, but they have been less dramatic than is generally supposed. The onset of double-digit inflation in the United States, for example, caused the dollar to plunge between 1977 and 1978, but, after adjusting for price changes, the year-over-year drop was only 9.6 percent—significant, to be sure, but hardly earth-shattering. As the Federal Reserve Board adopted an extremely tight monetary policy to fight inflation, the dollar appreciated by more than half between 1981 and 1985. Other currencies have also taken major swings: the value of the British pound, measured against the currencies of seventeen other industrial countries, rose 13.8 percent over a six-month period in 1986, then fell almost as much over the subsequent year, while Japan's yen climbed 39 percent in the twelve months ending August 1986.

These erratic exchange rate changes have not been as painless as advocates of floating rates had expected. But they have caused major economic dislocation only in the United States, and there only after a prolonged period in which the dollar exchange rate was far above its average long-term level. Not until 1984, four years after the dollar began its rise, did the resultant trade deficit become a major political issue in the United States. Had the currency's overvaluation been shorter-lived, its economic effects—and the political pressure to restructure the international monetary system—would have been far weaker. (Even then, exchange rates remained a mystery to the man on the street: a CBS News/*New York Times* poll in the spring of 1985 found that the public believed "a strong dollar is good for U.S. trade" by a margin of more than two to one.[10])

Steps to alter the international monetary system, then, need to focus on the fundamental question of long-term exchange rate alignment, rather than on curbing the activity of spot currency markets from one day to the next. Although exchange rate "instability" is often decried by those who would reform the system, daily price movements have relatively unimportant economic consequences. It is only when currencies remain misaligned for long periods of time that national economic authorities should be concerned.

Alignment and Misalignment

Economists with a strong faith in free markets dispute the notion that there is such a thing as "currency misalignment." Since in most cases the exchange rate is set by buyers and sellers in a free market, they contend, the market rate is more likely to reflect correctly the relative values of dollars, marks, and pounds than is some other rate established by the government. Even on a theoretical level, that argument is questionable, since there is ample evidence that human psychology, expressed through such terms as "gold fever," can cause market prices temporarily to reach levels that cannot be justified by sober analysis of supply and demand. It is equally questionable on a practical level, since there is really no completely "free" currency market. Central banks continue to hold foreign currencies and to buy and sell them in the markets whenever they are unhappy with their own nation's rate of exchange. They also deliberately seek to regulate the level of interest rates, which in turn directly affect exchange rates. As long as one or two central banks practice active exchange rate management, everyone else must as well: the alternative is not leaving exchange rates "to the market," but rather leaving them to the discretion of some foreign government.

But if the market price of the dollar is not necessarily the correct exchange rate, what is? Here, economists disagree dramatically.[11]

One school of thought suggests that exchange rates are "right" when a certain amount of money can purchase roughly the same amount of goods in different countries with similar levels of economic development, so that there is *purchasing power parity*. If a basket of typical consumer products costs $100 in the United States and 200 deutsche marks in West Germany, yet the exchange rate is only 1.7 marks per dollar, then the dollar is undervalued in terms of the mark. The correct policy response, advocates of purchasing power parity contend, is for U.S. and West German authorities to cooperate to push the dollar up or the deutsche mark down so that one dollar buys 2 marks, making the purchasing power of $100 or 200 marks the same in each country.

A second approach would arbitrarily set exchange rates in terms of some *"anchor"*—the price of gold, of a basket of commodities, or of some other international standard that could fill the role held by the dollar from 1945 until the early 1970s. The relationships between different currencies could be set according to purchasing power parity, current market exchange rates, or some other guide. Each government would be responsible for acting to keep that anchor stable in terms of its own currency, thereby stabilizing exchange rates as well.

The third major philosophy about exchange rates is that they should be at the level at which countries' current accounts— their trade plus their transfer of funds to foreigners—would be in balance. This so-called *external balance* approach rests squarely on the theoretical proposition that over the long run, whatever a country consumes from the rest of the world, through trade deficits and capital inflows, will have to be repaid. Exchange rates among countries at a similar level of economic development should, in this view, be at a level such that a nation's international accounts never get far out of line, eliminating the large changes in trade and investment flows from one year to the next that have proven so difficult for the world economy to handle.

Each of these approaches to determining the proper level of exchange rates without relying on the "free" currency markets has its shortcomings. The theory of purchasing power parity is conceptually faulty: because of differing transportation costs, trade barriers, market structures, consumer tastes, and endowments of resources, there is no particular reason why the cost of any given product should be the same across national boundaries. It is empirically wrong as well. The evidence of the 1980s is that purchasing power is rarely the same across national borders.

Moving to a gold or commodity standard begs the question of selecting the "correct" initial value for the anchor and, thus, for the exchange rates among dollars, marks, yen, and pounds—a basic problem with any fixed rate system. Nor does it offer a way for those currency relationships to change over time; past experience with fixed exchange rates indicates that the system will not survive unless currency values are able to change as one country experiences faster economic growth or a greater demand for foreign capital than another. As for the external balance approach, because almost every country's current account is out of balance each year, there is no way to know exactly what the "equilibrium" exchange rate is; the estimation is thus left in the hands of economists. Attempts to calculate this rate necessarily involve large margins of error and disagreements over arcane matters of theory.

Despite its shortcomings, however, the proposition that exchange rates should be at a level that allows each country to maintain its international accounts nearly in balance is probably the most useful guidance to officials in managing exchange rates. Although there is no economic reason why a nation's current account should be balanced at any particular time—countries have run current account deficits or surpluses for years on end, and developing countries requiring an influx of foreign capital need to be in deficit—every nation's trade in goods and international transfers of money balance out over the long haul. The external balance approach attempts to identify an exchange rate that minimizes the magnitude of the swings between current account surplus and deficit. Because those swings have real economic effects, such as turning labor shortages into labor gluts and making otherwise profitable investments suddenly uncompetitive, mitigating them may lead to a more stable economy. But the difficulty of determining exactly what exchange rate would bring a country's external accounts into balance—estimates of the "correct" relationship between the U.S. and Japanese currencies in late 1984 ranged from 131 to 198 yen per dollar, at a time when one dollar could buy 246 yen on the open market[12]—means that this approach should be used only as a rough guide for economic policy, not as a narrow target.

Targeting the Dollar

Since the Plaza Agreement of September 1985, in which finance ministers from the major industrial countries agreed on a concerted effort to drive down the international value of the dollar, it appears that estimates of the external balance exchange rates between the dollar, the yen, and the mark have served as targets to guide central bankers in managing exchange rates. By no means did central banks and their governments seek to drive the dollar overnight to a level at which the U.S. trade deficit would be eliminated. Instead, they encouraged the already skeptical currency markets to let the dollar fall gradually by nearly half over the thirty-month period between September 1985 and January 1988, allowing it to reverse course occasionally in order to discourage speculators from seeking to drive it down even faster.

During 1988, authorities in the United States, Europe, and Japan sought to stabilize the dollar in order both to allow time for European and Asian economies to adjust and to see exactly how much the U.S. trade deficit would cure itself. The governments concerned were faced with an uncomfortable trade-off: although few people believed that the dollar had fallen low enough to bring U.S. foreign trade back into balance, there was concern that the inflow of foreign capital required to fund the U.S. budget deficit would dry up unless exchange rates were stabilized. Their apparent response was to have their central banks buy and sell currencies in the market in order to hold their values within an agreed-upon trading range. This currency intervention was carefully orchestrated, involving close consultation among the Federal Reserve System, the West German Bundesbank, and the Bank of Japan.

The idea of formally establishing such multilateral cooperation in managing exchange rates has attracted wide support in business and academic circles. With the assurance that the exchange rates among key currencies would not be allowed to vary more than a small amount, the argument goes, investors and business people would be far more willing to make long-term commitments, knowing that a sudden change in exchange rates would not upset their plans. The European Monetary System, within which eight West European countries have agreed to cooperate to prevent their currencies from fluctuating more than 2.25 percent against each other (6 percent in the case of the Italian lira) with the provision for a negotiated realignment of exchange rates if existing ones become unrealistic, is often regarded as a model of how a new world monetary system might look.

But moving to a formal system designed to keep exchange rates within specified levels is neither a realistic nor a desirable step during the next few years.

A government's commitment to maintain the exchange rate of its currency is tantamount to saying that its currency's rate of exchange is its major economic objective. The major tool available to meet that objective is monetary policy: tighter money, raising domestic interest rates, increases demand for domestic currency and causes the exchange rate to appreciate, while easier money leads a nation's currency to lose value relative to others. If monetary policy must be fully committed to exchange rate stabilization at all times, it is not available for domestic purposes. A monetary policy to lower interest rates in order to stimulate domestic investment, for example, would not be permitted unless other countries chose to do likewise; if one country's interest rate were to be allowed to fall while others were not, the country would be violating its pledge to maintain its exchange rate.

In the context of the European Monetary System, where member economies are already closely tied to one another through participation in the European Community and will become even more tightly integrated in the next few years, a commitment to use monetary policy solely for exchange rate management is both economically sensible and politically feasible. Such a commitment is far less appropriate for the United States, given that trade with other industrialized countries remains a much smaller share of America's total output than is the case in Europe, and given a much lesser degree of economic integration with the rest of the world. Nor is it likely to be politically acceptable to direct the Federal Reserve to manage monetary policy solely to keep the exchange rate in line, without regard to the health of the domestic economy.

In any case, it is far from clear that governments have the economic knowledge to achieve a high degree of exchange rate stability within a floating rate system.

In the short term, central banks can move exchange rates by selling on the open market currencies judged to be "too high" and by buying those felt to be undervalued, thereby regulating the market price. Such intervention, however, is an expensive solution because of the enormous sums of money involved, and it is unlikely to prevail against market forces for long periods of time. An arrangement such as the European Monetary System provides one alternative, with the German mark serving as the key currency and other nations adjusting their policies according to whatever the West German central bank, the Bundesbank, chooses to do. But that approach is not relevant to the floating rate schemes now under international discussion, which would involve no key currency. Each country would be taking simultaneous aim at all other countries' currencies, requiring everyone, in effect, to hit a moving target in order to stabilize exchange rates—a feat of a much greater order of magnitude than is required within the European Monetary System.

Economic Coordination and Cooperation

Advocates of extensive exchange rate management without a return to fixed rates typically judge careful coordination of the economic policies of industrial countries to be the essential ingredient of stabilization. They would have the governments of major countries agree to hold exchange rates within a certain range, or "target zone," and to coordinate their monetary and/or fiscal policies if a currency's value threatens to go outside the agreed-upon range.[13] Even more ambitious proposals call for the governments in the leading industrial nations to continually monitor a set of economic indicators, such as national growth, inflation, and unemployment rates, and to intervene in predetermined ways if the indicators point in undesired directions.[14] In fact, the leaders of the industrialized countries have used just such a set of indicators to guide their joint policy on exchange rates, although they have eschewed the notion of automatic responses to economic events in favor of discretionary action.

Despite the extensive attention that international cooperation in shaping economic policy has received, the truth is that economists understand only poorly how policy coordination works in practice. The leading economic models are in sharp disagreement about such seemingly routine questions as the effect that expansionary monetary policy in the United States will have on other industrial economies, and diverge even more when it comes to such matters as whether an increase in a given country's government budget will cause its currency to appreciate or depreciate. Knowledge is certainly inadequate to allow the close coordination of day-to-day policy changes that exchange rate stability would require. And politicians are prone to dispute the opinions of the economic experts. Throughout 1983 and 1984, even as other countries were calling for the United States to help bring the dollar down, many Reagan administration officials publicly labeled the strong currency as a sign of economic strength and suggested that other countries, not the United States, make economic policy changes.

Target zones could be useful in curbing the most extreme fluctuations in exchange rates, while allowing the play of market forces to decide upon the level of rates within broad limits. The narrower the zones, the more frequently central banks will have to act to keep rates from exceeding the upper or lower bounds. To the extent that a quick purchase of dollars or sale of deutsche marks will move the market in the desired direction, target zones are relatively painless to maintain. But if markets' perception of the correct exchange rates is seriously at variance with that of the governments concerned, holding currencies within the desired range will require far more drastic action from each individual nation to adjust domestic interest rates against those abroad, either by manipulating the money supply or by altering fiscal policy. And if target zones are to be effective, governments will have to commit themselves, in advance, to taking whatever action is required.

From the American point of view, no president, Federal Reserve Board governor, or member of Congress is prepared to commit in advance to accepting the recommendations of other countries concerning U.S. economic policy. Few foreign governments will accede to such a system either. In practice, it would be difficult to forge international agreements that would obligate the United States to specific changes in fiscal policy, because the process of passing budgets and tax law changes is long and complicated; precisely the same factors that make it impractical to use fiscal measures to fine-tune the domestic economy make international fiscal policy coordination unworkable. Over the past several years, numerous international meetings on economic policy, including the annual economic summit of presidents and prime ministers from the seven leading market economies, have repeatedly called for major reductions in the U.S. budget deficit, but the Reagan administration proved unable to deliver on its commitments to do so. That leaves monetary policy as the only truly viable instrument that countries can use to achieve coordinated policy goals. Yet committing monetary policy to achieve internationally agreed-upon goals could be counterproductive for the United States. After finance ministers from major countries agreed at the Louvre meeting in February 1987 to stabilize the dollar, the Federal Reserve Board attempted to do its part by slowing down the rate of money supply growth, allowing interest rates to rise relative to rates in West Germany and Japan. The Fed's tight monetary policy, and fears that interest rates would have to go even higher to keep the dollar from falling, may be partly to blame for the investor jitters that led to the October 1987 stock market crash.[15]

Even if countries were to succeed in arranging their economic policies in a concerted fashion to keep exchange rates stable while maintaining noninflationary economic growth, the gains would likely be small. And if some policymakers should base their decisions on an incorrect model of the world economy, it is entirely possible that their coordinated actions could make the world worse off rather than better.[16]

Given the present state of knowledge, then, attempting to institutionalize policy coordination in a new international monetary system is not a desirable alternative. The flexibility in fiscal policy and the sacrifice of national monetary autonomy that would be required to stabilize exchange rates are just not in the cards. And reaching unsustainable agreements to stabilize the value of the dollar, as the major countries did at the Louvre, can be destabilizing when they fall apart, because the countries cannot agree on how to respond to changing circumstances.

This does not mean that the next president should turn his back on efforts to reach understandings on economic issues with major trading partners. Discussions of common economic interests among world leaders can be extremely helpful, especially when a country is about to embark on major changes in policy. Informing other leaders of changes of course can avoid the clash of dissonant policies among different countries and can allow leaders to raise objections to policies that they feel could be counterproductive for the stability of the world economy. Although the gains from formal agreements on exchange rates, growth targets, or policy changes may be small, efforts at cooperation are important because politicians may be unwilling or unable to force uncomfortable economic adjustments upon their constituents without commitments from other countries to take similar steps. Multilateral statements of policy offer evidence that other countries are sharing the burden of keeping the world economy healthy and growing, evidence that can help consolidate support for sound economic policies in the United States. But this is a far cry from seeking detailed agreement on each nation's domestic economic policies. In short, joint discussion of each government's intentions is all to the good, but turning discussion into coordination is going a step too far.

The greatest danger of relying on coordination to stabilize currencies is that it is all too easy to blame the economic policies of others for misaligned exchange rates and the resulting trade imbalances, rather than attending to economic problems at home. Restoring balance in the U.S. domestic economy, both by bringing government spending into line with revenue and by increasing private savings to meet investment demand, is a far more important goal than the difficult task of coordinating policies internationally to keep exchange rates stable.

Notes

1. William H. Branson and James P. Love, *The Real Exchange Rate and Employment in U.S. Manufacturing: State and Regional Results*, NBER Working Paper No. 2435 (Cambridge, Mass.: National Bureau of Economic Research, 1988).
2. John Williamson, *The Exchange Rate System*, rev. ed. (Washington, D.C.: Institute for International Economics, 1986).
3. Drawn from estimates in Rudiger Dornbusch and Jeffrey Frankel, *The Flexible Exchange Rate System: Experience and Alternatives*, NBER Working Paper No. 2464 (Cambridge, Mass.: National Bureau of Economic Research, 1987).
4. Ken Froot and Paul Klemperer, *Exchange Rate Pass-Through When Market Share Matters*, NBER Working Paper No. 2542 (Cambridge, Mass.: National Bureau of Economic Research, 1988).
5. Catherine Mann, "After the Fall: The Declining Dollar and Import Prices" (Paper presented to annual meeting of American Economic Association, Chicago, Ill., December 1987, mimeographed).

6. Paul Krugman, Robbins Lectures (Massachusetts Institute of Technology, 1988, mimeographed), pp. 2–7.

7. Lawrence Schembri, "Export Prices and Exchange Rates" (Paper presented to the National Bureau of Economic Research international trade conference, Cambridge, Mass., March 1988).

8. Martin J. Bailey and George S. Tavlas, "Trade and Investment Performance Under Floating Exchange Rates: The U.S. Experience" (Paper presented to Cato Institute monetary conference, Washington, D.C., February 1988, mimeographed).

9. For a before-the-fact exposition of the expected advantages of floating rates, see the comments of Milton Friedman in Milton Friedman and Robert V. Roosa, *The Balance of Payments: Free Versus Fixed Exchange Rates* (Washington, D.C.: American Enterprise Institute, 1967).

10. Clyde Farnsworth, "Most in Poll Found to Favor Import Limits to Protect Jobs," *New York Times*, June 9, 1985, pp. 1, 40.

11. For a discussion of the recent theoretical literature on exchange rates, see Marc Levinson, *Beyond Free Markets: The Revival of Activist Economics* (Lexington, Mass.: Lexington Books, 1988), pp. 99–116

12. Williamson, *The Exchange Rate System, op. cit.*, pp. 79–85.

13. On target zones, see Ibid; Jacob A. Frenkel and Morris Goldstein, *A Guide to Target Zones*, NBER Working Paper No. 2113 (Cambridge, Mass.: National Bureau of Economic Research, 1986); Gary Hufbauer, "Fiscal Key to Currency Reform," *Journal of Commerce*, November 12, 1987, p. 8A.

14. See, for example, John Williamson and Marcus Miller, *Targets and Indicators: A Blueprint for the International Coordination of Economic Policy* (Washington, D.C.: Institute for International Economics, 1987).

15. Martin S. Feldstein, "Distinguished Lecture on Economics in Government: Thinking About International Economic Coordination," *Journal of Economic Perspectives*, vol. 2, no. 2 (Spring 1988), pp. 3–13.

16. Jeffrey A. Frankel, "Obstacles to International Macroeconomic Policy Coordination," *Studies in International Finance* (Princeton, N.J.: Princeton University, 1988).

4

Debt and Development

The debt crisis, which began with Mexico's inability to service its enormous foreign debt in August 1982 and which quickly spread to other countries, shook the foundations of the international financial community. The crisis is largely over for the banking system, but for the developing countries it is no nearer its end than it was in 1982. Debt has continued to mount, and debtor countries are still strapped by heavy servicing charges and insufficient domestic investment. Even nations that undertook significant domestic reforms, such as Mexico, still are unable to sustain debt service obligations, and their economic growth continues to languish. At the same time, as bank loans have ceased to be available, the major international financial institutions, the International Monetary Fund (IMF) and the World Bank, have been withdrawing capital from debtor nations.

The debt crisis has had direct economic effects on the U.S. economy. As a result of the austerity programs imposed upon the indebted developing countries as well as the high dollar, U.S. exports to Latin America fell by $7 billion between 1980 and 1986. By one estimate, over 340,000 U.S. jobs were lost because of the decline in exports.[1] Meanwhile, U.S. imports from Latin America shot up as these countries struggled to earn sufficient foreign exchange to service their debts.

61

Until growth picks up in the debtor nations, domestic political turmoil is an ever-present possibility. And, if major debtors should refuse to service their debts, world financial markets would be seriously disrupted. Debt fatigue is setting in. The next president must explore new approaches to resolving the chronic crisis.

Beyond debt, America has diverse interests in developing countries, in which 77 percent of the world's population generates only 19 percent of the world's output.[2] Over one-third of U.S. exports go to, and almost 25 percent of U.S. foreign direct investment abroad is in, the developing world. Recent events in the Philippines, Central America, and Angola demonstrate the obvious security concerns. Rapid population growth in developing countries affects U.S. economic and security interests. World population passed the 5 billion mark in 1987 and another billion is expected before the end of the century. Over 90 percent of that increase will be in developing countries. The annual increment in population in developing countries is almost as large as the population of France and Spain combined. Larger populations represent potential markets for U.S. exports, but low per-capita incomes and higher poverty rates inhibit the capacity to import. An estimated 400 million people in developing countries—the absolute poor—do not have enough income to obtain the calories necessary to prevent stunted growth and serious health risks.[3]

As the only major industrial country to share a two thousand mile border with a developing country, Mexico, the United States has a unique interest in developing country issues. U.S.–Mexican economic relations are deeply entwined and profoundly influenced by labor conditions. Wages in Mexico are less than one-sixth those in the United States. Substantial underemployment exists in Mexico, where as much as 45 percent of the workforce is not fully employed. And the workforce is growing rapidly. Mexico would have to create up to one million new jobs annually between now and the year 2000 to absorb the new entrants to the labor force. But employment growth has been stagnant. With such depressed wages and a surplus of labor, the natural tendency is for Mexican goods to be exported to the United States and for U.S. investment to go to

Mexico. If domestic growth in Mexico does not provide enough jobs, however, then the incentive is for Mexican workers to migrate to the United States. American apprehension of illegal immigrants is running at record levels and is likely to increase in the future, especially if the debt crisis drags on.

Debt Debacle

Although malnutrition and poverty will remain U.S. concerns, debt is the number one problem in the developing world. It has both political and economic dimensions. Bank solvency and financial market stability could be at stake. Although creditors have had a rough time since 1982, it has been even rougher for the debtors.

Latin Americans speak of the 1980s as a "lost decade" in which growth has stagnated, real incomes have declined, and human suffering has increased. The years of austerity and suffering are starting to undermine confidence in the democratic governments that took power in most Latin American nations in the 1980s.

In the wake of the 1988 Mexican election, in which the ruling party lost ground to opponents calling for reductions in debt payments, opposition candidates challenging for the presidency in Argentina, Brazil, and Venezuela are charging that debt service burdens condemn their countries to misery. Debt service as a percentage of exports is running over 20 percent in several countries, and it is above 40 percent in Argentina (see Table 4). This saps funds that could be used to invest in, modernize, and expand local industry. Between 1981 and 1986, the proportion of gross national product devoted to investment in Latin America sank from 24 percent to 16 percent.[4] Output per capita in Latin America is unchanged from ten years earlier. And to the extent that these countries must run trade surpluses, national output exceeds national expenditure and living standards suffer further.

How did this happen? During the 1970s and 1980s, many developing countries borrowed heavily abroad to expand their industrial capacity but also to finance balance-of-payments deficits caused by an extremely volatile world economy—high oil prices, falling commodity prices, and surging interest rates—

Table 4
The Major Debtor Countries in Latin America

Country	Total Debt* ($ billions)	Interest Payments (as a % of exports†)
Argentina	$62.7	41.3%
Brazil	120.2	30.1
Chile	21.5	17.9
Colombia	17.7	21.2
Ecuador	11.1	27.9
Mexico	107.3	27.9
Peru	18.8	37.5
Venezuela	34.7	23.4

Source: Institute of International Finance, Washington, D.C., as reported in Roger Cohen, "Latin's Head Toward Harder Debt Stance," *Wall Street Journal*, July 22, 1988, p. 19.

* 1988 year-end forecast.

† Estimated

and to cover domestic policy errors, such as chronic fiscal deficits and overvalued exchange rates that served as incentives to overspending and capital flight.

In the 1970s, commercial banks, flush with recycled petrodollars, actively competed for clients in developing countries with loans tied to prevailing interest rates in New York and London. But when the worldwide recession of the early 1980s brought plummeting commodity prices and double-digit interest rates, the cost of servicing outstanding debt sharply increased. Banks abruptly cut off lending to most developing countries, leaving many nations on the brink of default.

The approach to resolving the debt crisis has gone through three phases and it entered a fourth in December 1987.[5] At the outset, in 1982 and 1983, the fear was that the international banking system would collapse. To avert a financial panic, the U.S. government, the International Monetary Fund, and the commercial banks successfully collaborated to assemble rescue packages that postponed the payment of loan principal and provided new flows of capital in exchange for austerity programs in the debtor countries. After three years of austerity programs and case-by-case rescheduling, Secretary of the Treasury James A. Baker III in 1985 declared that growth should be emphasized instead of austerity, and that new money and later more resources for the multilateral institutions would be made available for countries that undertook significant domestic reforms. The second stage was launched.

When a year and a half passed without the desired growth and without new money from the commercial banks, it became evident that the "Baker Plan" had stalled. Creditors became increasingly unwilling to extend new loans. U.S. banks continued to reduce their exposure in Latin America, and governments made no effort to fill the gap. Reflecting a general loss of confidence, the value of Latin American debt in secondary markets plummeted.

The third stage began in the summer of 1987, when the U.S. Treasury quietly started to promote a "menu" of options such as local currency payments and the conversion of loans into equity at deep discounts. A foreign investor who wants to buy assets in a debtor country first buys, at a discount, some of the country's debt and then swaps the dollar-denominated debt for the local currency, which, in turn, is used to finance a direct investment in fixed assets or equities. These debt-equity swaps have grown into a $5 billion to $8 billion market. But it seems unlikely that the vast majority of the debt—in excess of $1.2 trillion—could be converted into equity and sold. Such an invasion of foreign investors would be politically unacceptable in many debtor countries, and can also contribute to inflation.

The fourth stage was reached in December 1987, when, for the first time, the U.S. government agreed to back a debt-relief package. The U.S. Treasury and the Mexican government developed a plan under which the commercial banks could exchange some of their long-term, public sector loans to Mexico at less than face value for new Mexican long-term bonds, with the principal collateralized by Mexico's purchase of U.S. Treasury bonds. While the response by the commercial banks to the Mexican plan was lukewarm, debt relief seems to be making its way into the menu of options for the middle-income debtors. (In the summer of 1988, the U.S. government finally agreed, after prodding from other industrial countries, to a debt-relief and forgiveness package for the low-income African debtors.)

There are important political reasons why the debt should be a major concern in Washington. U.S. diplomatic relations with the developing world have suffered because of the economics of debt. Politically, it appears as if a massive, perverse redistribution of income is taking place. Latin America has transferred $145 billion to foreign creditors over the last six years. Indeed, the Soviet Union has mounted a propaganda offensive in Latin America pointing out this perversion. Many of the indebted developing countries are fragile democracies and cannot risk enduring austerity much longer. If political turmoil erupts, their future history books could place the blame on democracy and debt. Political instability would also increase the probability of a multicountry default, which could precipitate a crisis in financial markets.

What can be done about it? The current approach, aptly called "muddling through," envisages a continuation of frequent rescheduling agreements between creditors and debtors, with possible new wrinkles such as those introduced in 1987 and 1988: debt-equity swaps, exit bonds, the lengthening of maturities, and the lowering of spreads. This approach is preferred by U.S. commercial banks. To the banks, no change in strategy is needed because the financial system has not collapsed and they have "bought" time to improve their balance sheets.[6]

But five years of belt tightening have failed to revive the economies of many developing nations, debt reschedulings have become more difficult, and lenders remain extremely reluctant to extend new credits. The danger that desperate debtor nations could act unilaterally is still present. Some banks remain overexposed and could become insolvent if debtor countries banded together, formed a cartel, and stopped payment. Further confrontations between debtors and creditors would erode U.S. diplomatic relations with these developing countries.

These conditions have prompted several proposals to establish an international fund to purchase a portion of the outstanding debt at substantial discounts with subsequent readjustment of debt-service burdens on a country-by-country basis. Reduced debt service would allow the countries to use more of their export earnings for investment to spur growth. Proponents argue that a comprehensive solution would have the benefit of solving the crisis and of enabling countries to concentrate on domestic economic management. It would also provide a longer-term framework for commercial banks and might even allow the recovery of a greater proportion of their outstanding loans than if they continued to seek full repayment.[7]

It is hard to envisage the circumstances under which such a grand scheme could happen, however. At the least, it would take years to initiate and would be complex to administer. It could also inadvertently harm the credit ratings of other developing nations and possibly involve serious losses for banks. Industrial countries would have to contribute large-scale financing, while taxpayers in those countries might wonder why their taxes were being sent to countries whose own taxpayers sent money abroad. Furthermore, if the new debt facility were tied to the World Bank or the IMF, as most proposals are, it could compromise their financial standing and transform them into debt collection agencies, rather than providers of aid and temporary financial assistance.

In any discussion of the debt crisis and its possible resolution, the two critical variables are interest rates and exports. As long as export earnings are growing at a rate higher than the prevailing interest rate, debt/export ratios are stabilized and debt servicing is manageable. If the interest rate exceeds the growth in exports, as it did in 1981–83, and the country still borrows all it needs to cover its servicing obligations, the debt/export ratio will rise and at some point become unsustainable.[8]

So, as a rule of thumb, countries should aim to have their export earnings rise to a degree that at least matches the rate of interest. Expanding exports in most countries requires more investment, and that means more borrowing. At present, however, the investment inflows required to boost exports are being used up by the need for imports of parts and components and the need to service the debt. The countries are being constrained by insufficient foreign exchange from their export earnings and investment inflows.

Therefore, it is important to keep interest rates down. Responsible fiscal policies in the United States could have a significant impact on interest rates. Since most of the loans are based on floating rates, a decline in U.S. interest rates could help ease the debt-service burden.

Although the debt crisis is a multilateral problem, changes in U.S. bank regulations may be needed. For example, one way to protect debtors from a run up in the interest rate would be to cap the floating rates. Banks, of course, would be reluctant to do that unless the interest payments in excess of the cap were added to the principal. This would help debtors by putting a lid on the quarterly interest payments, but does allow the banks to recover the excess over the longer term. There is an uncertainty, however, as to how regulators would treat such deferrals. If they counted against their earnings, banks would not establish interest caps. Clarification of regulatory policy could pave the way for banks to use interest capping as a means of sharing the risk more equitably between debtors and creditors, and it could be very much in the banks' own interest. The one thing that could inspire the formation of the dreaded debtor cartel would be a sharp increase in interest rates. A cap would minimize the chances.

Changes in U.S. banking law to adopt provisions similar to U.S. bankruptcy law could also be beneficial. Up to 2,000 banks were involved in the 1987 Mexico restructuring. Many of the medium-sized U.S. banks were reluctant to pour in additional funds. Unlike domestic bankruptcies, where agreement by an effective majority of the creditors is sufficient to force a court-ordered solution, agreement by all creditors is required to restructure loans to foreign governments. Enormous persuasion is needed to get smaller banks to put up additional money. They would prefer to be free riders. Who can blame them? After all, why put up $1 to get $2 if you can put up nothing and get the same return? Changes in domestic laws might help to get domestic banks to go along in restructurings.

Expanding developing country exports, of course, will require growth in the industrial countries. But it will also require a shift in the source of that export growth. From 1982 to 1986, the United States was the developing world's best customer, taking over 60 percent of its manufacturing exports compared with 30 percent by the European Community and less than 10 percent by Japan. Without U.S. purchases, the indebted countries might fall into default. Other countries will have to absorb more of the developing countries' products in the years ahead. The United States, which will need to run a surplus of its own in trade, cannot continue as the major purchaser.

The debt crisis can be solved only with better policies in the debtor countries, a large increase in external capital flows, and a new international framework for handling the situation. Better policies are always the condition for restructuring existing debts and for new money. What has been lacking is new external capital flows. Indeed from 1985 to 1987, $30 billion in resources flowed out of the middle-income indebted countries.

Five general guidelines should be followed for a new approach on debt. Initial negotiations over debt relief should be done on a case-by-case basis; the approach should be voluntary and market-oriented; the debtor country must develop a policy package in consultation with the IMF and the World Bank and accept greater surveillance by them; conventional criteria for bankruptcies should be revised, and some bank regulatory changes could help spread out losses; and, finally, creditor governments or the international financial institutions should be used to back interest, and perhaps principal, on bonds in those cases where significant restructuring and debt relief are required.[9]

U.S. budget deficits preclude major infusions of new government money, and since it would appear to be a bailout for the commercial banks, the politics is not right. Japan could play a greater role in guaranteeing debt restructuring, but, like other countries, it could have more impact by contributing its money to the World Bank where such capital infusions are multiplied by the Bank's ability to borrow from international capital markets.

The debt crisis will not go away, and the next administration often will be forced to make decisions piecemeal, as in the Mexican agreement. The United States, however, cannot solve the problem on its own. Any solution that puts renewed emphasis on growth will have to be a multilateral one involving the various creditor countries. There is simply no alternative but to have the international financial institutions play a greater role. This raises the question of what role the IMF and World Bank should play in coordinating a response, and what the U.S. posture toward these international financial institutions should be.

Initiatives by International Institutions

The international financial institutions are comprised of the World Bank, the IMF, and three regional institutions—the Inter-American Development Bank, the Asian Development Bank, and the African Development Bank. In the 1980s, these institutions have become a major source of controversy in the U.S. Congress, especially when increased funding for them is up for consideration on the floor. On the one hand, some conservatives object to their loans to leftist governments. On the other, some liberals see the legislation for increased funding as an opportunity to pursue favorite causes, such as assisting the poor and protecting the environment.

The World Bank and the IMF were the outgrowth of efforts in the late 1940s to bring order to a world wracked first by the Great Depression, and then by World War II. These institutions were designed to oversee international finance and to transfer resources to the less well-off.

The World Bank lends at near-market rates to middle-income countries, and at easier terms to poorer countries. Annual lending now exceeds $17 billion. The World Bank's concessional loan window, the International Development Association, is the single-largest source of foreign capital for the poorest countries, including those in Sub-Saharan Africa. Loans support both investments in development projects as well as structural reforms aimed at making developing economies more efficient.

The IMF provides temporary financial assistance to countries with balance-of-payments problems. These countries typically are required to reduce budget deficits, devalue their currencies, and undertake reforms aimed at correcting economic imbalances, without resorting to inefficient government interventions and restrictive trade practices.

The United States played a critical role in the founding of these multilateral institutions and it has benefited from their existence in a variety of ways. First, the development banks provide finances directly to development projects that purchase U.S. products; they, therefore, act to generate jobs in the United States. Second, the institutions foster growth and increase purchasing power in the developing world, thus the markets for U.S. products expand. Finally, they generally advocate an open, liberal international economic system, which benefits U.S. commercial interests.

The international financial institutions, however, have often received an ambivalent reception from both the Congress and the administration, because they lack a constituency and they are not always seen as promoting U.S. interests. A central concern for Congress and the administration is the degree to which the United States controls the multilateral institutions. In the World Bank and the IMF, votes are allocated in rough proportion to levels of contribution. The United States is the dominant member in both, holding approximately 20 percent of the votes—enough to veto major policy changes. In the forty years since the Bank and the IMF were created, the U.S. share of total contributions to them (and its corresponding share of the vote) has steadily decreased. A principal American goal has been to encourage other major countries to take up the slack by increasing their level of contributions as a way of sharing responsibilities. Thus, successive administrations have faced a dilemma: they have sought to maintain or increase U.S. influence while asking other countries to provide more of the required funding.

If these international financial institutions are going to help resolve the debt crisis and are to be prepared for the financial challenges of the 1990s, the United States must take the lead in revitalizing them. Of course, doing so will take more resources, but not much more. With the support of the Reagan administration, the World Bank is seeking a major capital increase of about $75 billion. If it contributes 20 percent, and 3 percent is paid in (the remainder being covered by guarantees), the United States would provide roughly $450 million over five years. The legislation necessary for this increase is being held up by members of Congress who contend that a more comprehensive and credible approach to the debt problem is required.

America's interests in the health of the World Bank are often overlooked. Its exports to World Bank projects exceeded $1.6 billion in 1987, which is more than the $1.5 billion it has made in direct cash contributions over the institution's forty-year history. For each dollar the United States provides in the general capital increase, the World Bank will be able to lend more than $200.[10] That is quite a bang for the buck.

The Inter-American Development Bank does not have quite the same impact, but at $40 for every dollar donated, it, too, creates large multiples of contributions. If it were fully funded, it would amount to less than $100 million in outlays over five years. The Inter-American Development Bank is vitally important for resolving the debt crisis because its membership includes all of the Latin American debtors.

The IMF also is likely to seek a major increase in funding within the next few years. An expansion of IMF resources, known as quotas, would not be a direct budgetary expense for the United States, because it is done as a government guarantee. Quotas are the credit lines that can be drawn upon when countries are experiencing balance-of-payments difficulties. Other IMF resources consist of gold, national currencies, and Special Drawing Rights, a form of international money created in the 1960s to provide additional liquidity for the global economy. No increase in Special Drawing Rights has been made since 1981. A special issue of Special Drawing Rights, equivalent to expansion in world monetary aggregates like gold, distributed to the neediest developing countries would not result in any direct budgetary outlays and could provide a badly needed infusion of capital for those countries.

Increasing resources for these international financial institutions, even when no budgetary authority is involved, has proven to be contentious in Congress in the past. Whenever separate bills were introduced, they became the focal point for amendments and debate. A host of restrictions on U.S. voting behavior at these institutions has ensued, such as laws requiring U.S. representatives at the banks to oppose loans to countries that violate human rights, that expropriate U.S. property, that provide refuge to terrorists, and that create new competition for U.S. producers.

Often the best way to get the legislation for increased resources to these institutions passed through Congress was to put it in a huge omnibus bill or in the continuing resolution needed to fund government operations. This could change if two new approaches were adopted. First, a persuasive case needs to be made that the United States is going to campaign to get the World Bank and the IMF to shift their emphasis from austerity toward assisting the indebted countries in servicing their debts and the impoverished countries in building infrastructure. Second, expansion of the institutions needs to be presented as a package. Indeed, as C. Fred Bergsten has proposed, there are advantages to having Congress consider them in such a manner.[11] In a package, they are more likely to get the thoughtful attention they deserve and since members of Congress find it painful to decide in favor of such legislation, it minimizes the number of times they have to vote.

Over the longer haul, more substantial changes in the roles of the IMF and the World Bank would be desirable. The IMF needs to put more emphasis on medium-term adjustment. Its normal stand-by arrangements to provide balance-of-payments financing are intended to last for only one year, which is too short a time for fundamental policy reforms to take hold. Three years would be better. This will require that more funds be shifted into the IMF's modestly funded Extended Fund Facility.

Second, the IMF should devise new ways of lending to governments when payments shortfalls are caused by events out of the control of the local government. This has been done on a small scale—for instance, when there has been a drop in export prices—but not in the cases of a rise in interest rates, which increases debt-service costs. If such events could be seen as cause for seeking IMF assistance, then governments might be more willing to apply for IMF funds and to accept the institution's recommendations for policy reform. As it now stands, countries delay turning to the IMF until the last minute, because they want to avoid the political fallout from such reform. If they applied earlier, then the reforms would be less drastic.[12]

Long-term reform of the World Bank could be more substantial. Although it needs to remain vigilant about retaining its credit rating, the Bank should sharply increase its level of disbursements to the main debtor countries and assert its leadership in handling the problem from here forward. More of its resources should be allocated to its structural adjustment loans. The quid pro quo for receiving structural adjustment loans should be more far-reaching domestic policy changes. The Bank should also stand ready to guarantee or to facilitate exit bonds, as with the U.S.–Mexico agreement in December 1987. The World Bank, if nothing else, can act as a catalyst to activate governments and lenders to participate. If such programs draw deeply upon the Bank's resources, then another general capital increase may be needed. But since the general capital increase proposed in 1988 was expected to last until 1998, another one in the mid-1990s should not be much of a problem if the world economy is able to avoid the Sword of Damocles hanging over its head because of the debt crisis.

Finally, the World Bank could conduct a special capital increase by accepting contributions to its reserves from the surplus countries—notably Japan and Germany—in exchange for more voting power. This would be another component of the necessary effort to share responsibilities in the world economy. With the U.S. share of total contributions in a steady decline, America is now close to losing its veto power, but too much should not be made of the veto. Even if its share fell below 15 percent, the United States certainly could get another country to go along with a blocking action. And the United States has never used its veto to date anyway. Alternatively, the Bank might consider establishing a special facility for recycling Japanese surpluses, as the IMF did for Saudi Arabia in the 1970s.[13] New initiatives such as these are going to be necessary to solve the debt crisis and to get the international financial institutions ready to deal with the economic problems of the 1990s.

Foreign Aid's Future

U.S. assistance to multilateral institutions is only a small portion, and a declining one at that, of U.S. foreign aid. The justification for U.S. foreign aid policies has been varied: security, commercial, ethnic, historical, and humanitarian. And the focus has shifted over time from cold war politics and development, to human rights concerns and, in this decade, back to military assistance. Foreign aid lacks a strong constituency on Capitol Hill; Congress is very reluctant to vote for foreign aid bills and often complies only by attaching provisions that severely constrain the administration.

Outlays for foreign aid at the end of the Reagan administration are unchanged on a constant-dollar basis from when the president took office.[14] (The outlays for different categories are broken down in Table 5). Over one-third of all aid goes to Egypt and Israel as part of the U.S. commitment to the Camp David peace accord. The component that has increased the most since 1981 is the Economic Support Fund, which provides bilateral economic assistance usually associated with short-term political or strategic objectives. On the other hand, outlays for multilateral aid after adjusting for inflation declined by 42 percent between 1981 and 1988. Assistance under the Food for Peace Program (P.L. 480) also declined, but that program traditionally varies with changes in weather conditions and crop prices at home and abroad. Only aid to Israel and Egypt and economic support funds are now at higher levels in constant dollars than they were during the Carter administration.

The general direction of U.S. foreign aid in the 1980s has been to deemphasize aid's role as a tool of development, leaving the humanitarian and security objectives as the principal rationale for such programs.[15] The shift toward security and away from economic development assistance has been so marked and the programs have become so muddled that it prompted two close observers to ask "Should the bilateral foreign aid programs of the United States in the 1980s be regarded as an element in its foreign economic policies or as a tool for propping up economies considered vital to U.S. military security?"[16] And the administration was not forthcoming on new multilateral initiatives. Its unwillingness to join most other industrial countries in contributing to a special $8 billion fund for impoverished African countries in 1986 represented a new low in U.S. support for multilateral aid efforts.

Table 5

Composition of U.S. Foreign Aid

(*% of total*)

Type of U.S. Foreign Aid	1981	1987
Bilateral development	18%	17%
Food for Peace	13	10
Multilateral aid	13	10
Economic Support Fund	4	12
Military aid	7	7
Egypt and Israel	36	36
Greece, Portugal, Spain, and Turkey	9	8

Source: Joel Johnson, "Foreign Aid: The Reagan Legacy," Overseas Development Council *Policy Focus*, no. 2 (1988).

President Reagan's original emphasis in administering foreign aid was to support U.S. security interests abroad. By the mid-1980s, however, the administration could no longer count on either an expanding federal budget or a public willing to rise to the call of anticommunism. Although the president continued to invoke the communist threat as the justification for U.S. aid, the threat cited was usually specific to particular countries, rather than as a general consequence of economic backwardness. In addition, aid programs began to assign the private sector as large a role as possible. Privatization became a widespread theme.[17]

At the same time, Congress reached new heights in its attempt to have a voice in U.S. foreign policy through its power over the purse. Congressional committees, in their efforts to reduce the budget, began eliminating provisions that lacked substantial domestic support and attaching unprecedented numbers of amendments to the aid legislation. Floor debates over foreign aid began to turn into general debates on the administration's foreign policy agenda. The proposed inclusion of family planning support in U.S. aid efforts in 1984 caused a lengthy debate about overpopulation and birth control, the implications of which went far beyond the aid program under discussion. As another example, President Reagan's 1985 request for assistance to El Salvador stimulated a congressional review of the administration's Latin American policy; and, in the process, Congress delayed passage of the aid legislation. The search for a domestic drug enforcement policy also affected the aid bills of the 1980s, with U.S. assistance to several countries made contingent upon their ability to curb the production of drugs within their own territories.[18]

The coalition of those concerned with development and humanitarian objectives in winning American foreign aid is no longer effective. It has been unable to compete against the constraints of the U.S. budget and the clamor of the power struggle between Congress and the president over broader foreign policy goals. Critics assert that the U.S. foreign assistance program has been effectively eliminated, replaced by thinly disguised efforts to bolster American military allies abroad, expand Third World markets for U.S. goods, and further other U.S. objectives not shared by the aid recipients. The program is viewed as chaotic and incoherent.

Clearly, the time has come for a full-fledged review of American aid programs. The last major review was in 1973; the next president should conduct a new one and propose new legislation. As the current administrator of the Agency for International Development put it after reviewing the governing statutes, he was "appalled" by the law's unwieldiness.[19]

Even in an era of budgetary constraint, it is possible to get more out of the aid budget in terms of U.S. economic and humanitarian interests. Greater use of government guarantees to stimulate private financing and a shift to more multilateral aid are two examples.[20] Getting other countries to step up their support for Third World development would be another.

The United States does not stand alone with its assistance programs for the developing countries. Although the United States is the largest donor of official development assistance, on an absolute dollar basis, it is second from the bottom as a share of gross national product (see Table 6). In 1986, the United States only contributed 0.23 percent of gross national product

Table 6
Who Gives the Most Foreign Aid?

Country	% of GNP (1986)	$ billion
Norway	1.20%	$0.80
Netherlands	1.01	1.74
Denmark	0.89	0.70
Sweden	0.85	1.09
France*	0.72	5.11
Belgium	0.49	0.55
Canada	0.48	1.70
Australia	0.47	0.75
Finland	0.45	0.31
Germany	0.43	3.83
Italy	0.40	2.40
United Kingdom	0.32	1.75
Switzerland	0.30	0.42
New Zealand	0.30	0.08
Japan	0.29	5.63
Ireland	0.28	0.06
United States	0.23	9.56
Austria	0.21	0.20
All these donors	0.35	36.70

Source: Organization for Economic Cooperation and Development figures as published in Bretton Woods Committee, "Special Report on Japanese Aid" (Washington, D.C., 1988).

Note: Figures are for official (government) aid to developing countries.

* Including aid to French possessions. Excluding such aid, France's ratio of aid to GNP is 0.49% and its assistance totals $3.51 billion.

for official development assistance. Japan did not do much better, at 0.29 percent. Now that it has become the world's largest creditor nation and with its continuing surpluses, international pressure is building for Japan to step up its aid and lending to developing countries.

Broadly construed, aid and security assistance can be seen as international public goods, like welfare programs and police forces are domestically. Since Japan's constitution prohibits it from spending more than one percent of its national income on defense, Japan should devote more of its resources to assisting developing countries, and without the provision that they spend the money in Japan.[21] In response to such pressure, Japan has announced a $50 billion foreign aid plan over five years, which would make Japan the world's number one donor. This is roughly double the aid Japan authorized in the previous five-year period.[22] When calculated in yen, however, this increase appears less dramatic, because the yen has appreciated substantially against the dollar. Japan's aid expenditures would still be only about 0.35 percent of gross national product, which is the average for the industrial countries. In addition to restructuring U.S. aid programs, the next president should encourage Japan to increase its foreign aid. Sharing the responsibilities in this area would be most welcome.

An Opening for Trade

One sure way to raise the standard of living in developing countries is through expanded trade. Industrial and developing countries seek greater access to each other's markets. The developing countries, particularly the upper-tier, newly industrialized countries, the oil-producing nations, and, until recently, the high-debt Latin countries have been the most rapidly growing markets for industrial country exports. But most developing countries still have vast pools of underutilized resources with unemployment and underemployment rates running as high as 40 percent to 45 percent. If trade could be liberalized and these resources were to become employed, income and trade would expand rapidly.

Today's children are tomorrow's workers, and population developments are reshaping the world labor force and the patterns of demand which will last well into the next century. Out of every one hundred people added to the world's population in the next twenty years, ninety-five will be born in the developing world and only about five in the industrial countries. The implications for trade are immense. Competitive pressures on world markets will increase as the developing countries' need for new jobs and incomes climbs rapidly. At the same time, the enormous investment needs and consumer demand in the developing countries could make them the world's most dynamic markets in the years ahead.

Integrating the developing countries more fully into the trading system could provide a big boost to world growth. Employment of the surplus labor in developing countries would increase output and growth in much the same way as surplus labor was absorbed after World War II. The largest contribution to growth in the postwar period resulted from the shift of resources from less productive to more productive sectors. Most trade between industrial and developing countries is complementary. Industrial countries export capital goods and import consumer (labor-intensive) goods.[23] Today, a shift from consumer goods to capital goods production in industrial countries, along with less reliance on protection in capital goods sectors in developing countries, could pay growth dividends. At the same time, open markets would encourage all countries to specialize in areas in which they enjoy advantages and not try to produce every possible good and service.

If negotiations led to extending developing country access to all industrial countries, both sides would benefit and the world economy would receive the growth stimulus it so badly needs. Unfortunately, however, the industrial countries have many sticks and few carrots to encourage the developing countries to negotiate. The adjustment problems in industrial countries are most pronounced, and the political power is greatest, in the labor-intensive sectors in which the developing countries are most competitive. It is in these sectors in which existing measures, tariff and nontariff barriers and the "voluntary" restraint agreements, are the most restrictive.[24] Perhaps some of these restrictions could be removed through trade talks.

Notes

1. Overseas Development Council, *Agenda 1988: Growth, Exports and Jobs in a Changing World Economy* (New Brunswick, N.J.: Transactions Books, 1988), Annex B-8, p. 234.

2. A useful compendium of analysis and statistics on U.S. interests in the developing countries is *The U.S. Economy and the Developing Countries*, compiled by Richard Feinberg and Gregg H. Goldstein for the Overseas Development Council as briefing papers for the presidential candidates, Washington, D.C., 1988.

3. *Agenda 1988, op. cit.*, Annex D-6, p. 263.

4. Bradley Graham, "No Quick End in Sight for Latin Debt Malaise," *Washington Post*, April 12, 1988, p. C3.

5. Shafiqul Islam, "Breaking the International Debt Deadlock," *Critical Issues*, no. 2 (1988), Council on Foreign Relations, New York.

6. For a synopsis of the pros and cons of different approaches to debt, see Richard Feinberg and Christine A. Bogdanowicz-Bindert, "Third World Debt," in Feinberg and Goldstein, *The U.S. Economy and the Developing Countries, op. cit.*

7. See, for example, James D. Robinson III, "Weaving a Debt Net," and Eugene H. Rotberg, "Toward a Solution to the Debt Crisis," both in *The International Economy*, vol. II, no. 3 (May/June 1988), pp. 50–55 and pp. 42–49, respectively. Senator Bill Bradley (D, N.J.), one of the earliest to recognize the significance of the debt issue and to propose comprehensive reform, has held extensive congressional hearings on debt. See *The Impact of the Latin American Debt Crisis on the United States* and *The Third World Debt Problem*, hearings before the subcommittee on International Debt of the U.S. Senate Finance Committee, March 9, 1987, and April 6, 1987, respectively.

8. See Tim Congdon, *The Debt Threat* (Oxford and New York: Basil Blackwell, 1988).

9. Shafiqul Islam, "Debt Deadlock," *op. cit.* He argues that "the simplest and most effective option seems to be to induce the banks to pass through their income and capital losses into debt relief by allowing them to swap their risky, floating-rate, longer-term, public sector loans for safe, marketable bonds with long maturities (fifteen to thirty years) and coupon rates fixed below market rates. These bonds could be issued directly by the debtor government seeking relief, with the principal as well as interest guaranteed by a major creditor government."

10. Bretton Woods Committee, *Banking on Success: The World Bank, the United States and the Developing World*, Washington, D.C., 1988.

11. C. Fred Bergsten, *Foreign Economic Policy for the New Administration and Congress* (Washington, D.C.: Institute for International Economics, forthcoming, 1988).

12. For critical comments and suggestions on conditionality and structural adjustment, see E. L. Bacha, "IMF Conditionality: Conceptual Problems and Policy Alternatives," and P. Streeten, "Structural Adjustment: A Survey of the Issues and Options," both in *World Development*, vol. 15, no. 12 (December 1987), pp. 1457–68 and pp. 1469–82, respectively.

13. Richard Feinberg, et. al., *Between Two Worlds: The World Bank's Next Decade* (New Brunswick, N.J.: Transaction Books, 1986).

14. See Joel Johnson, "Foreign Aid: The Reagan Legacy," *Policy Focus*, no. 2 (1988), Overseas Development Council, Washington, D.C.
15. John Sewell and Christine Contee, "Foreign Aid and Gramm-Rudman," *Foreign Affairs*, vol. 65, no. 5 (Summer 1987), pp. 1015–36.
16. Raymond Vernon and Deborah Spar, *Beyond Globalism: Remaking American Foreign Ecomomic Policy* (New York: Free Press, 1988), p. 141.
17. See Raymond Vernon, ed., *The Promise of Privatization: A Challenge for U.S. Foreign Policy* (New York: Council on Foreign Relations, 1988).
18. For extensive review of the recent history of the foreign aid programs, see Vernon and Spar, *Beyond Globalism, op. cit.*, chapter 7.
19. Christopher Madison, "Overhauling Foreign Aid," *National Journal*, May 28, 1988, pp. 1410–12.
20. Sewell and Contee, "Foreign Aid," *op. cit.*
21. Bela Balassa and Marc Noland, *Japan and the World Economy* (Washington, D.C.: Institute for International Economics, 1988).
22. Clyde Haberman, "Japan, Under Pressure, Is Raising Foreign Aid," *New York Times*, June 15, 1988, p. 12.
23. C. Michael Aho and Jonathan D. Aronson, *Trade Talks: America Better Listen!* (New York: Council on Foreign Relations, 1985 and 1987), chapter 3.
24. For a discussion of the politics of protection and sectoral problems, see Robert Baldwin, "U.S. Trade Policy Since World War II," in Robert Baldwin and Anne O. Krueger, eds., *The Structure and Evolution of Recent U.S. Trade Policy* (Chicago: University of Chicago Press, 1984), and the references therein.

5

Trade Talks or Trade Tangles?

Resisting protectionism at home while minimizing trade frictions and liberalizing trade abroad will be a top priority for the person who occupies the White House in January 1989. U.S. trade policy has fundamentally changed under the Reagan administration, despite its free trade rhetoric. As a result, trade frictions with other countries are likely to multiply during the term of his successor.[1]

Trade is a complex policy issue, standing as it does at the intersection of foreign policy and domestic economic policy. Trade negotiations are conducted between national governments, but they simultaneously involve domestic negotiations among diverse interest groups. Although nations as a whole gain from freer trade, not every individual is better off. Domestic adjustment is painful. Firms and their workers do not move effortlessly to sectors favored by open trade. The negative consequences of increased import competition are concentrated and are felt immediately, while the gains from a wider variety of products and lower prices are diffused and come with delay. Complicating matters further are the U.S. trade remedy laws that grant domestic interests hurt by surges in imports or unfair foreign trade practices an almost automatic right to relief and, with it, the ability to manipulate trade policy. The challenge facing policymakers is to balance continually these diverse interests.

The U.S. trade deficit began the decade in 1980 at $24 billion and grew steadily to $171 billion in 1987. Imports rose by over 63 percent, while exports were essentially flat, increasing by only 13 percent, and then not until 1987. The deterioration of the trade deficit resulted from both the appreciation of the dollar, which acted like a tax on U.S. production and a subsidy for foreign production, and the strength of the domestic economy compared to that of Western Europe and the heavily indebted developing countries. And, as imports shot up, the number of private sector complaints under the trade remedy laws mushroomed from fifty-eight in 1980 to 103 in 1985 before leveling off in 1986 and 1987.[2]

The large trade imbalance and vociferous private sector complaints have spawned unprecedented administrative and legislative action on trade. In September 1985, after four years in which it repeatedly labeled the trade deficit a sign of economic strength, the administration changed course and began vigorous, if not always effective, action against allegedly unfair practices by foreign firms and foreign countries. It initiated over a dozen unfairness complaints against countries accused of maintaining barriers to U.S. exports. Despite its free trade orientation, the Reagan administration negotiated quotas on imports of carbon steel, machine tools, and semiconductors. According to Treasury Secretary James A. Baker III, the Reagan administration has provided more import relief than any of its predecessors in the past fifty years.[3]

The Reagan administration's record on trade has not been entirely negative. It was U.S. pressure that was crucial in launching the current Uruguay Round of multilateral trade negotiations, under the auspices of the General Agreement on Tariffs and Trade (GATT), in which ninety-six nations are trying to reach an accord on issues not now covered by international trade rules. In addition, the administration concluded a free trade agreement with Israel and an historic pact eliminating tariffs and reducing barriers between the United States and Canada. But, on balance, during the Reagan years, U.S. trade policy has become more tit for tat and protectionist.

Disputes among trading partners over specific policies are neither new nor particularly worrisome. What is unusual and troublesome about trade problems today is that they escalate quickly into highly politicized issues involving "zero-sum" diplomacy. Increasingly, trade policy is viewed as a strategic game in which national economic gains can be reaped only at another country's expense. This view, which is reinforced by the increased use of bilateral negotiations to resolve disputes, stands in sharp contrast to the postwar perspective that trade provided mutual gains to trading partners. Frictions have been and will continue to be acute with the major pillars of the trading system, Japan and the European Community.

Despite the decline of the dollar, the United States will persist in pressing Japan on trade. Trade policy in the United States is loser-driven, with the least successful firms calling the shots. And there is always the chance for a "coalition of the frustrated." Legislators representing those industries in direct competition with Japan—beef, citrus, rice, telecommunications, and automobiles, among other products—may one day band together to vote unilateral action against Japan. Those legislators are anxiously waiting for positive action from Japan, yet increases in its imports of U.S. products have come slowly and grudgingly.

But Japan may be less able or less willing to accede to American demands in the years ahead. The combination of a rising currency, rapid technological change, and the widespread movement of Japanese firms offshore could result in labor adjustment problems within Japan, just as similar changes did in the United States. Will Japanese domestic harmony and consensus be strained by the combination of these events? If the Japanese unemployment level rises, adjustment problems will be exacerbated. And even without adjustment problems, an intense resentment is building in Japan, especially among the younger generation, in response to feelings that the country is being pushed and bashed by the Americans.[4]

Trade relations with the European Community are unlikely to be better and could even get much worse. As the Community moves toward 1992, when it intends to become a truly common market, it will continue to struggle with its financially burdensome policy of subsidizing farm production and will increasingly be plagued by regulatory inconsistencies. The factors that explain Europe's difficulty in adjusting are familiar: record unemployment, the lack of a unified market, the pervasive role of the government in many countries, limited wage and labor market flexibility, and the fragility of coalition governments that requires government leaders to tread carefully. Ideally, the Community should eliminate barriers among its twelve members while simultaneously liberalizing market access for foreign firms, but it is more likely to protect against foreign interests while it liberalizes internally.

A unified, thriving European Community is as much in the U.S. interest today as it was thirty years ago. If the internal market reforms are carried out as scheduled, the output of the Community could rise by 5 percent, allowing its member states to buy more from the rest of the world and pay a greater share of the North Atlantic Treaty Organization's (NATO) defense bill. The open question, however, is whether unification will lead to an increase in European protectionism, to further discrimination against outside interests, and to a greater use of subsidies to keep troubled industries alive. If that happens, U.S. exports will suffer, and trade tensions will escalate.

The biggest source of trade frictions, however, could be the substantial deterioration in other countries' trade balances, as the United States shifts from a trade deficit of $171 billion to a surplus of as much as $40 billion to $50 billion over the next decade. If other countries try to resist, trade frictions could get much worse. A swing of this magnitude would be easier to accomplish if world trade is expanding; if a recession should strike, however, trade tensions would be exacerbated.

Trade frictions can be handled multilaterally, bilaterally, unilaterally, or in some combination of the three. The United States has been the champion of multilateralism and nondiscrimination in trade ever since 1934, when the fragmentation and eventual breakdown of the trading system were identified as contributing to the length and severity of the Great Depression.

A number of lessons can be learned from the experience of the 1930s. First, retaliation and discrimination can feed the growth of protectionism worldwide. Second, when changes in the levels and forms of protection are unpredictable, it is very risky for businesses to import parts or to build new plants. Third, heavy losses in output and employment occur when investment is reduced and directed into less-rewarding projects. Fourth, protection breeds protection, and beggar-thy-neighbor policies are self-defeating because they end up impoverishing all countries. Finally, the 1930s made clear that trade policy conflicts resulting in a decline in trade and output can provide fertile ground for political radicals to seize the reins of government. The multilateral trading system drawn up after World War II was an attempt to protect against a repetition of these catastrophes.

Today, the trading system is once again on the brink of fragmentation and the United States is groping to find its way on trade policy. Sentiment is growing for the United States to abandon its traditional multilateral approach to trade and to forge bilateral and regional agreements with like-minded countries. Alternatively, the United States could unilaterally adopt a tit-for-tat aggressive trade policy, retaliating against alleged unfair trade practices or against countries that maintain persistent surpluses. Or the United States could turn inward, erecting, brick by brick, a wall of trade restrictions to stem the flow of imports. Each of these alternative approaches has benefits and costs compared with a global bargain achieved through multilateral negotiations.

Multilateralism

The General Agreement on Tariffs and Trade is the multilateral institution that provides the rules and procedures under which international trade is conducted. When those rules and procedures are followed, uncertainty is reduced, which allows international investment, trade, and growth to expand. The GATT is one of the three major international institutions designed to help stabilize the world economy in the post–World War II environment. But it does not have the authority in trade that the International Monetary Fund has in finance, or that the World Bank has in development. The GATT is an administrative agency with a professional staff of fewer than two hundred people. Its role is to facilitate negotiations and to resolve disputes, not to actively manage the world trading system.

The GATT was intended to help remove quotas and reduce tariffs and other barriers to trade in goods. The centerpiece of the GATT system is the principle of unconditional "most-favored-nation" treatment or nondiscrimination, which prohibits countries from playing favorites. In addition, trade-restricting actions are supposed to be overt, not covert, with prior consultation with trading partners.

Today, however, the international trade rules embodied in the GATT are no longer adequate.[5] A shrinking portion of world trade, primarily that in manufactured goods, falls under GATT jurisdiction, and even that portion is not handled very well. Governments no longer abide by, or even agree upon, the rules that should regulate trade. Important issues, like services and investment, are not covered. In contrast to the earlier period, the trend in the trading system is toward fragmentation, not integration. New initiatives are needed to prevent further disintegration of the system. It is now only a slight overstatement to say that the GATT has been overtaken by events. If present trends continue, it will not be an overstatement at all.[6]

In the face of these challenges, progress in the multilateral negotiations is necessary to begin to restore confidence in the fairness and efficacy of the trading system. This is vital if governments around the world are to resist protectionist pressures: only when the protective structure is examined as a whole do the diffuse gains from trade liberalization become large enough for the political process in each nation to resist new restrictions demanded by those who lose from more open markets. Negotiations provide a way for organizing the political will to push the trading system forward. Ongoing negotiations give policymakers something to point to in resisting the requests of special interests for protection. Only in the context of a major round of negotiations do affected private interests favoring freer trade mobilize and lobby effectively.[7]

The Uruguay Round of multilateral negotiations, named for the country that hosted the meeting of trade ministers at which it was launched, began in September 1986. According to the declaration announcing the new round, the talks are to be completed by 1990. Achieving that ambitious timetable is unlikely. The last multilateral talks under the GATT, the Tokyo Round that concluded in 1979, exceeded their deadline by more than two years.

The Uruguay Round negotiations are taking place against a dark background of increasing barriers to international trade. In the words of the GATT "Wisemen's" group, assembled to study the trading system, "Today the world market is not opening up; it is being choked by a growing accumulation of restrictive measures. Demands for protection are heard in every country, and from one industry after another."[8]

Pressures for trade restrictions abound, because unemployment has been high, by historical standards, in Europe, Japan, and, until recently, the United States. They will increase because of the labor adjustment problems inherent both in heightened international competition and in the transition to highly automated manufacturing. As the global economic imbalances are eliminated and the U.S. trade deficit diminishes, pressures for protection will become more intense in those countries that will see their trade surpluses becoming deficits, particularly in Europe and East Asia.

Yet, even as the trading system faces great dangers, opportunities are evident. The developing countries, the fastest-growing markets for industrial country exports, still have vast pools of unemployed or underutilized resources. Integrating them more fully into the trading system will be the greatest challenge of the coming decade. If this can be accomplished, the world economy would get a sorely needed boost to growth, comparable to the one it enjoyed after World War II when the United States used its dominant economic power to promote trade liberalization. For over a generation, from 1950 to 1973, the world economy experienced unprecedented growth, averaging 3.3 percent per annum. Trade liberalization was a major factor creating that growth and helped to spread it around the world.

The issues being discussed in the Uruguay Round include the unfinished business of previous trade rounds, such as subsidies and nontariff barriers; strengthening the system, by bringing sectors such as agriculture, textiles, and steel more fully under the auspices of the GATT; extending GATT rules to new areas such as services, investment, and intellectual property; and institutional reform, such as improved dispute-settlement procedures. The United States is one of the foremost proponents of new agreements on most of these issues, particularly extending the GATT to cover new areas.

The new administration is unlikely to achieve any quick results. Apart from the decline in U.S. influence and willingness to take the lead in opening markets, which makes cooperative action imperative, several other factors will make the current negotiations more difficult than earlier trade rounds. First, a larger number of countries are playing a critical role in the negotiations. Second, growing interdependence makes the distinction between domestic and international economic policies obsolete. Third, the world has entered an era of higher unemployment and slower economic growth. And, finally, there is a practical problem, too: trade negotiators lack the political authority in their own countries to strike deals in many of the areas, such as agriculture and services.

The new administration should stand firmly behind the effort to enhance and update the GATT. To the extent possible, difficult problems that are now handled outside of the GATT must be accommodated within it. Otherwise, the credibility of the system will continue to erode. Several institutional reforms are needed.

Dispute-settlement procedures need to be more uniform and timely, and disputants must be convinced that they should abide by decisions. The GATT secretariat should be granted sufficient authority to publicize trade restrictions and violations of GATT commitments, and to call meetings to debate actions by offending countries. In order to examine trade and finance issues in a more consistent manner, GATT oversight should be more closely coordinated with the World Bank and the International Monetary Fund.

The increased pluralism in the world economy has created decisionmaking problems for the GATT and threatens to politicize the organization, turning it into another forum for airing North-South issues. The consensus decisionmaking of the GATT could prove its undoing unless a streamlined process can be agreed upon. The creation of an ongoing consultative process or even an executive committee to replace the present system of irregular meetings would help the GATT function more decisively.

As a growing force in international trade, the developing countries need to be brought into the bargaining process of GATT. They are now accorded special treatment through preferences and exceptions, and are not required to make reciprocal concessions in negotiations. In short, the industrial countries treat them differently. If they are willing to accept greater responsibilities, they will acquire more rights and exercise' more positive influence. To get them to bargain seriously, however, the industrial countries will probably have to grant them enhanced access to their markets.

Finally, the role of state-trading and nonmarket economies in the world trading system needs to be the focus of U.S. attention. With China already negotiating for membership in the GATT and the Soviet Union waiting in the wings, the Uruguay Round might provide the last opportunity to redefine the responsibilities of nonmarket economies. In other cases, the GATT has adopted a results-oriented approach to nonmarket economies; when Poland joined, it agreed to increase imports by 7 percent per year. With regard to China and the Soviet Union, however, the United States should insist that they agree to trade strictly on a commercial basis. This would require published rules for granting import licenses, transparency in decisionmaking, and more meaningful price systems. The Soviet Union's petition to join the GATT is not likely to come up until after the completion of the Uruguay Round. It would be better to clarify these issues now than to try to negotiate them after a petition is filed.

Achievement of institutional reforms to ensure that trade issues are dealt with more promptly would be a significant accomplishment, but it will not be sufficient to quell the growing disdain on Capitol Hill for GATT and multilateralism. A stronger system cuts both ways. The United States will have to agree to adhere to GATT rules and principles when they go against U.S. interests, as well as when they support them.

To restore the credibility of multilateral negotiations as a way of solving problems, concrete results will be needed on subsidies, market access in high-technology goods, agriculture, services, and intellectual property, or on some portion of the above. The development of codes governing services trade, counterfeiting, and intellectual property is possible even if immediate liberalization is elusive. Progress on subsidies and agriculture will be more difficult. And, in order to gain greater market access in high technology, the United States will probably have to permit greater market access for textiles, steel, footwear, and apparel from developing countries. If a sufficiently large package of trade-liberalizing measures and new rules cutting across most of these issues cannot be developed, the administration will have a hard time winning congressional ratification.

Europe could be a problem. Negotiators from other countries will be hard-pressed to come up with something to attract the European Community. Its resistance to a stronger, more legalistic GATT system is long-standing and unambiguous. The Community prefers ad hoc political deals. Agricultural subsidies are the glue that holds it together, making a major agreement on farm trade unlikely in this negotiating round. It will be extremely difficult to form a European position favorable to liberalization of trade in areas such as telecommunications and insurance until the 1992 effort at internal restructuring is completed.

Japan could be a key player as the GATT talks progress. Japan has benefited most from the open trading system and now will have to bear more of the responsibility for its maintenance. With the highest growth and the lowest unemployment of the major industrial countries, Japan is in the best position to liberalize its markets. The United States should encourage the Japanese government to establish a set of broad targets for import penetration of the Japanese market over time, and then meet them. Unless purchases of foreign goods and services increase, pressure on Japan in bilateral and multilateral arenas will remain intense.

The strongest developing countries, such as South Korea and Singapore, will also have to accept more responsibilities for maintaining the trading system. They will be asked to pay their fair share. These countries would clearly benefit if GATT is strengthened and market access in industrial countries is increased. In return, they would have to give up their preferential treatment and provide more market access themselves, both to industrial countries in capital-intensive goods and to the least developed countries in labor-intensive products. In addition, the United States should insist that they accept some general principles on services, and stricter rules on counterfeiting and intellectual property.

Progress negotiating so many issues among so many countries will be painstaking and slow, particularly if some countries drag their feet. In order to put pressure on reluctant or recalcitrant countries, bilateral alternatives may need to be explored.

Bilateral Alternatives

The distinction between bilateral and multilateral approaches is not necessarily one between bad and good or darkness and light.[9] While bilateral agreements in textiles and steel restrict trade, other agreements are trade-expanding. Bilateral agreements that invite others to join, to abide by stronger rules, and to share in the benefits, can be useful in promoting greater certainty in international commerce. On those issues not covered by international rules, such as investment practices, progress can often come only through bilateral negotiations.

Bilateral and multilateral approaches do not exhaust all the possibilities. Regional or plurilateral agreements are another approach. Some of the codes agreed to during the Tokyo Round negotiations apply only to those countries willing to accept stronger rules and procedures. For example, only firms that are signatories to the government procurement code may bid on government projects in other countries that are open to foreign bids. Such limited agreements can be useful in putting pressure on countries that are free riders or foot draggers. More comprehensive bilateral agreements can also be a prod to the multilateral process.

If the multilateral talks should flag, the Reagan administration has proposed to negotiate a series of bilateral free trade agreements or to establish a "club of free traders." This proposal comes on the heels of the administration's successful negotiation of a bilateral free trade agreement with Canada, our largest trading partner.[10] (A less-comprehensive agreement was negotiated with Israel in 1985.) The administration deserves credit for successfully negotiating the pact with Canada, because it did signal that trade liberalization remains possible and that international negotiations can still bear fruit. The Canadian pact has gone further, faster than the multilateral GATT round, and it could be a catalyst for those talks. In fact, that was, from the U.S. perspective, their major purpose.[11] Additional bilaterals, however, could result in increased trade frictions and could eventually fragment the trading system.

Bilateral agreements are justified only in special cases. Israel and Canada are special cases. President Reagan in his 1988 State of the Union address spoke of including Mexico in a North American accord. Mexico may also be a special case—although the Mexicans themselves have evidenced little interest—but after that, it is hard to see the Congress and the private sector in the United States going along with any other bilateral free trade agreements.

Other countries surely would object. Resentment would prevail among outsiders. Inefficiency would be spawned by the fragmentation of markets. Bureaucratic nightmares would result for the government and private firms trying to cope with the discrimination among countries. And foolish signals would be sent to those policymakers in developing countries who are proponents of free markets and multilateralism. After Canada and Israel, and aside from an agreement with Mexico sometime in the next century, the options are spent.[12]

Discriminatory bilateral agreements cannot combine to form a globally consistent, stable system of national trade policies. Such a system requires effective equality of rights and obligations among countries, which can be ensured only by general acceptance of the principle of nondiscrimination or most-favored-nation treatment. With bilateral or like-minded groupings, some countries inevitably will be left out. How will they be chosen and who will decide? In this country, Congress will have to play a role. Consider how its members will be whipsawed by country interests and the desires of individual industries. Legislative action on separate agreements also opens up the possibility that trade will be used as a weapon of foreign policy against countries that are not following in lockstep with the United States. If so, the next president would find himself spending more time on the balance of trade, leaving him less time to spend on the balance of terror. That would be a gross misallocation of resources.

Bilateral or like-minded agreements also will smack of colonialism to left-of-center politicians in many developing countries. Even for those given preferential treatment, such an arrangement would add fuel to domestic political battles in those countries, to say nothing of the domestic political battles in countries whose exports would be subject to discrimination.

The major pillars of the trading system, the United States, Japan, and the European Community, cannot afford to be in rival blocs. Although, the United States has expressed frustration with the European Community for slowing the multilateral process and with Japan over market access, Western cooperation remains important also for strategic and security reasons and must not be undermined. The best message of security cohesion nations with market economies can send to Eastern bloc nations is a flourishing, unified, nondiscriminatory trading system. A fragmented trading system, with friction and discrimination, would send the wrong signal.

And, if the trading system should fragment as a result of a misguided bilateral strategy, how will the United States be able to generate trade surpluses of up to $50 billion to service a trillion-dollar foreign debt in the 1990s? Without an open multilateral trading system, that will be next to impossible. Before the trading system self-destructs, efforts to strike a multilateral bargain should be redoubled.

Unilateralism and the Next Trade Bill

As he struggles to contain trade frictions with our trading partners abroad, the new president will also have a domestic negotiation to contend with on trade matters. The Constitution specifically empowers Congress to "regulate foreign commerce." The president's ability to negotiate credibly with other countries comes from the delegation of negotiating authority from Congress. Then, after a package is negotiated, it must be submitted to Congress for ratification. But passage of a trade bill extending the authority to negotiate or to implement trade agreements always comes at a price.

In the past, both types of legislation have been accompanied by other policy changes that Congress demanded as its condition for supporting trade liberalization. In the case of the Trade Expansion Act of 1962, Congress revised U.S. trade laws and passed the first trade adjustment assistance program for workers. And because Congress felt that the State Department was giving too much weight to foreign policy considerations in its trade negotiations, it created a new office in the Executive Office of the President, the U.S. Special Trade Representative, to serve as trade negotiator and as a broker between domestic interest groups and with Congress.

With the passage of the Trade Act of 1974, which authorized the president to participate in the Tokyo Round of multilateral trade negotiations, Congress rewrote U.S. trade laws on unfair trade practices, including cases involving foreign subsidies or dumping, lowered the threshold for injury to firms, and substantially liberalized adjustment assistance for workers. And in the Trade Agreements Act of 1979, which implemented the agreements reached in the Tokyo Round, Congress went even further in removing presidential discretion in the unfair trade statutes and in transferring the responsibility for enforcing the laws from the Treasury Department to the Department of Commerce.

Congress passed a trade bill in 1988 which was unprecedented in size and in scope. It ran 497 pages in length, and over twenty congressional committees had a role in drafting it over a three-year period. In addition to traditional trade remedy legislation, it covered everything from export promotion to developing country debt. The 1988 legislation makes it easier to obtain import relief and reduces the president's flexibility in resolving trade disputes.

From the next president's perspective, the important thing in the 1988 legislation was the delegation of negotiating authority until May 31, 1991. Under the "fast track" provisions of the bill, Congress agrees to consider within ninety days any agreement reached and no amendments are in order. This gives the president credibility in negotiating with other countries. If no agreement is reached by May 31, 1991, "fast track" will expire and any agreements will be subject to delay and amendment. This deadline will be useful for reaching an agreement in the Uruguay Round, but the president will still have to negotiate with Congress, either to get an extension or to agree upon implementing legislation.

When he must submit new trade legislation to Congress, the next president should try a new approach—one designed to maximize U.S. leverage with its trading partners. The biggest threat the United States has, and often the major factor motivating other countries to action, is the prospect that Congress might pass protectionist legislation. Why use that leverage only before negotiations begin and again at their conclusion? If Congress, in its delegation of negotiating authority, were to establish intermediate deadlines, it could stipulate that any agreements reached on those dates contain contingency clauses that would abrogate them if further progress were not forthcoming in the negotiations. This would certainly increase U.S. bargaining power in multilateral talks.

The establishment of deadlines compels the administration to take action on trade policy issues. Other countries make a point of using top-level political officials to intervene in trade disputes. In the United States, executive branch leaders rarely focus upon trade issues unless they are forced to by Congress. As deadlines approach, trade invariably receives higher-level political attention. Deadlines force decisions, and forcing clear decisions about U.S. trade policy goals would mark a major change for the better.

Another desirable change in U.S. trade legislation would be to improve the information on the costs and benefits of trade restrictions. Disraeli once remarked that in international trade, there are no principles, only interests. The problem is not that all interests are heard from. Furthermore, in most public discussions of trade protection, the right questions seldom are asked. If legitimate issues of adjustment or national security are involved, are import restrictions the most efficient policy available? The primary consequences of trade restrictions are felt by different groups within countries, not between countries. Better information on the consequences would help policymakers to make better-informed judgments. The GATT Wisemen's report recommended that all countries develop and adopt a protection balance sheet or a protection impact statement to improve internal trade policy formulation.[13] In its next trade bill, the United States should require such impact statements. This could be done by expanding the mandate of the International Trade Commission.

At the same time, U.S. trade laws should be reoriented toward pressing other countries to open their markets, rather than toward protecting domestic industries. There should be more emphasis upon deterrence and retaliation for the purpose of strengthening adherence to the internationally established rules of trade.[14]

The importance of deterrence is invariably neglected in discussions of international economic affairs, although it is elemental in understanding strategic relations among nations. From the viewpoint of advocates of free trade, tolerating offensive behavior without retaliation is an admirable form of self-restraint. But its effects on other nations' trading practices can be unfortunate. Tolerance signals America's commitment to maintain a liberal trading order, but it also signals that other countries may be able to infringe upon the rules without prosecution. Retaliation, far from being something to avoid at all costs, is a necessary part of a self-regulating world system of free trade.

The rules of the GATT were deliberately written to discourage actions that could erupt into trade warfare. As a result, a country establishing import barriers that would violate GATT rules knows in advance that retaliation, if any, would do no more than take away whatever benefits its illegal trade policy may reap and, given the slowness of GATT procedures, would also be several years in coming. The probability that a country illegally interfering with trade will suffer major economic harm from retaliatory action is very low. Deterrence is negligible.

This reluctance to retaliate is also enshrined in American trade law. Although the U.S. government frequently imposes sanctions against trading partners, those sanctions almost always come with protectionist rather than market-opening intent.

Indeed, the administration of the antidumping and countervailing duty statutes is almost like an entitlement for complaining firms. An alternative approach stressing retaliation against foreign actions that violate multilateral trade rules is needed. But retaliation should be reserved for practices that are clearly at variance with the internationally defined rules of the world trading system, and, in each instance, the United States should define clearly and state publicly what action on the other country's part will cause the U.S. retaliatory measures to be lifted. It must be limited to selected cases: if every foreign practice alleged to violate the rules of international trade is made the subject of retaliation, the United States will be involved in an endless series of trade disputes, many of them of minimal economic consequence.

In addition, retaliation should occur only within the realm of international trade, to make it clear to others that the United States has no desire to allow trade disputes to poison other aspects of its international relations. Trading partners should be confident that eliminating the objectionable practice would bring an end to U.S. interference with their exports. Meeting this condition will require substantial changes in U.S. laws, which now allow individual companies and industries to file for import relief with little cost and no risk, and which require the government to grant relief if certain conditions are met. These provisions allow individual companies, particularly those that are least able to compete in the international economy, an inordinate influence in setting U.S. trade policy, and they strip American trade diplomats of much of their bargaining leverage: a trading partner has little incentive to make compromises to avert retaliation when it knows that any individual company can still obtain sanctions against it. Perhaps some of the current laws could be traded away in the Uruguay Round and replaced by a specific policy of retaliation, granting the president the flexibility to impose and withdraw retaliatory penalties.

A frank policy of retaliation against foreign barriers would also provide visible evidence to the domestic political arena that the U.S. government is vigorously asserting the country's interest in trade matters. This will help establish presidential credibility on trade, greatly diminishing protectionist pressures in Congress.

Some steps in this direction have already been taken, and the 1988 trade bill emphasized market-opening retaliation over market-closing protection. Increased use of retaliation against foreign barriers might help to forge new rules in the context of the multilateral talks. The publication of foreign trade barriers to U.S. exports, as required by law, and the occasional public disclosure of lists of retaliation targets can also have the effect of deterring the further spread of barriers. If new barriers are erected, then some items on the list of retaliatory targets could be publicly indentified in order to mobilize the public sector in the offending country.[15]

Applying deterrence to trade policy does carry with it the risk of escalation, retaliation, and counterretaliation. Some of this risk can be avoided by carefully selecting the targets for retaliation. This requires a competence and an objectivity on the part of the officials in the executive branch both in choosing barriers to retaliate against and in selecting the targets of retaliation. Although it offers one possible means of maintaining a self-enforcing system of international trading rules, this approach requires well-defined rules that are lacking today, and the ongoing multilateral talks under the auspices of the GATT provide the best opportunity to improve the rules that govern trade.

Trade Tactics

A great deal needs to done to reform the international trading system. It will not be easy and it will not happen overnight, but the stakes are too high not to keep trying.

Each country has strong forces pushing it to protect its narrow interests and its most vocal interest groups. Yet, the system could collapse if it is torn apart by each nation pursuing its own short-term interest. The world is now so interdependent that it is impossible to isolate any economy from the whole. If protectionism replaces efforts to achieve freer trade, the effects will be felt everywhere. If the trading system crumbles, as it did under the weight of depression and protectionism in the early

1930s, no country will escape. In short, nations will either work together to revitalize the system now or pay the price if nationalistic trade policies bring the system down.

As the next U.S. administration struggles to find its way on trade policy, the world will wait nervously. The next president will have to take the initiative selectively if he wants to stem congressional frustration and to open foreign markets. Trade can no longer be treated as a stepchild of domestic economic policy at home and of foreign policy abroad. It must be a continuing priority. For if U.S. leadership on trade waivers or falters, other countries will pick up the cue and efforts to move forward will be undermined. America's next president must mobilize private sector support and must push hard for progress in the Uruguay Round. Progress will be essential for maintaining the credibility of negotiations as a way of solving problems. But progress will become more difficult as other countries' trade accounts deteriorate.

Transitions from one administration to another are always difficult in American foreign policy. Much, if not all, of the institutional memory is lost as one group of policymakers leaves and another takes over. But the transition in 1989 may be uncommonly difficult on trade policy.

The Reagan administration has been negotiating in more arenas than ever before, from bilateral steel and textile quotas to patent protection in developing countries, from restrictions on Japanese semiconductors and machine tools to the sweeping bilateral accord with Canada. Many of these negotiations are extremely detailed and very labor-intensive to conduct. How will this web of sectoral, bilateral, and multilateral agreements be passed on to the next administration? Will anything be lost in the transition? That worry alone should lead the next administration to step back and question the wisdom of conducting such a labyrinth of negotiations that in many cases are inconsistent with one another.

Because of this complexity and the need for concrete results in the ongoing multilateral talks, the president must appoint a trade negotiator with experience covering the issues and with familiarity with the major players at home and abroad. The president must make clear that he has confidence in and will actively support his trade negotiator, as President Carter did with Robert Strauss. Above all, the next U.S. Trade Representative will have to have substantial political acumen to cope with the looming problems in sensitive sectors.

Notes

1. C. Michael Aho, "More Trade Frictions Lie Ahead," *Journal of Commerce*, May 12, 1988, p. 8A.
2. These figures combine petitions under the escape clause, antidumping, and countervailing duty statutes. They are derived from the appendix tables in I.M. Destler, *American Trade Politics: System Under Stress* (Washington, D.C.: Institute of International Economics/New York: Twentieth Century Fund, 1986).
3. Remarks by Treasury Secretary James A. Baker III, Institute for International Economics, Washington, D.C., September 14, 1987.
4. Ellen Frost, *For Richer, For Poorer: The New U.S.–Japan Relationship* (New York: Council on Foreign Relations, 1987).
5. For an examination of the challenges confronting the GATT and what might be done about them, see Miriam Camps and William Diebold, *The New Multilateralism* (New York: Council on Foreign Relations, 1983 and 1985).
6. But we should not forget that the success of the GATT also contributed to more harmonious international political relations. Since the GATT was founded, there has been no world war, and today war between France and Germany is virtually unimaginable. Furthermore, democratic values are taking root in Spain, Portugal, and several Latin American countries. It is difficult to distribute credit for these successes between the GATT, the Marshall Plan, the formation of the European Community, NATO, and the use of active macroeconomic policy to avoid the disastrous economic slumps of earlier periods. In any event, harmonious trade policy allowed other issues to occupy the attention of foreign policymakers. In that way, the GATT played a critical, although largely unseen and unappreciated, role.
7. C. Michael Aho and Jonathan D. Aronson, *Trade Talks: America Better Listen!* (New York: Council on Foreign Relations, 1985 and 1987).
8. *Trade Policies for a Better Future: Proposals for Action* (Geneva: GATT, 1985), p. 1.
9. For an analysis of how bilateral and multilateral approaches interact, see William Diebold, "The History and the Issues" in William Diebold, Jr., ed., *Bilateralism, Multilateralism and Canada in U.S. Trade Policy* (Cambridge, Mass.: Ballinger Publishing Company/New York: Council on Foreign Relations, 1988), pp. 1–36.
10. For an assessment of the U.S.–Canadian free trade agreement, see William Diebold, "The New Bilateralism" in Diebold, *Bilateralism, Multilateralism, op. cit.*, pp. 128–92.

11. C. Michael Aho and Marc Levinson, "A Canadian Opportunity," *Foreign Policy,* no. 66 (Spring 1987), pp. 143–55.

12. C. Michael Aho, "Most Bilateral Trade Pacts Carry a Penalty," *Wall Street Journal*, March 18, 1988, p. 26.

13. *Trade Policies for a Better Future: Proposals for Action, op. cit.,* pp. 35–37.

14. Marc Levinson, "Trade Policy or Trade Strategy" (Working Paper for a Council on Foreign Relations study group on the Economic Choices Confronting the Next President, New York, May 10, 1988, mimeographed).

15. I. M. Destler and John S. Odell, *Anti-Protection: Changing Focus in United States Politics* (Washington, D.C: Institute for International Economics, 1987).

6

The Sensitive Sectors

Within the broad array of trade problems confronting the next administration, the question of government supports for specific sectors of the economy will be among the least tractable. In their preoccupation with maintaining industries judged critical to economic vitality or national defense, and in their eagerness to help constituents who fear economic change, politicians in almost all countries have created a web of subsidies and supports for certain favored parts of the economy. This ever-widening variety of assistance programs has become a major international issue, and for good reason: by altering the flow of international commerce, they block the economic forces that should lead countries to focus on producing the things they make most efficiently and inhibit the course of economic change.

Certain industries, among them steel, agriculture, and ship-building, benefit from government aid in almost every country around the world. The result has been a seemingly permanent state of surplus capacity: although the supply of steel plate or winter wheat or container ships may outstrip demand for years on end, leading to free market prices so low that producers cannot recover their costs, no individual producer has reason to depart the business as long as the government is willing to pay the losses. Instead, producers continue to churn out things for which there is a market only thanks to further government intervention, such as donations of food to poor countries or restrictions on competing imports. In other sectors, notably apparel and shoes, the natural advantages of low-wage developing countries have been counteracted by protectionist policies in industrial nations that interfere with the flow of trade. In both cases, each country pushes the problems caused by its subsidies and support programs onto others.

The inefficiencies inherent in maintaining uncompetitive industries amount to a major waste of America's economic resources, dragging down the standard of living. In many cases, they cause a serious drain on the federal budget as well. Both the difficulty of maintaining living standards and the budgetary constraints the United States will confront in the decade ahead make it imperative to reduce the level of support to individual industries—a step that will prove politically feasible only as part of an agreement by which other countries do the same.

While the question of subsidies is supposed to be dealt with as part of the broader talks under the auspices of the General Agreement on Tariffs and Trade (GATT), the inability of the GATT members to reach agreements on the issue during past negotiations leaves little ground for optimism. In addition, some major economic powers—notably the European Community, which has used cross-subsidy schemes to bind its twelve members closer together, and whose officials derive much of their power from their ability to pass out money—are notably unenthusiastic when the talk turns to curbing subsidies. Whatever real progress can be made is likely to come outside the GATT. Strong leadership from the United States, including the personal involvement of the president, will be required if other nations are to take American proposals seriously—and if they are to believe that the United States is prepared to act on its own if they fail to respond.

Government supports for individual industries, regions, or groups of workers are nothing new. Tariffs, taxes on foreign goods, are a common way to subsidize domestic producers against import competition; many countries also have made special efforts to subsidize exports. As the volume and scope of international commerce have grown, however, the line between domestic measures and those affecting international commerce has blurred. Government programs that were once considered to have purely domestic purposes now have consequences abroad as well as at home. Multinational corporations structure their operations internationally to maximize profits worldwide, so a subsidy that assists a company's operations in one country can easily alter its competitive position elsewhere. In addition, technology has led to a dramatic change in the cost structures of many industries in which international competition is widespread. Whether the product is a prescription drug, a bond underwriting, or a piece of software, the cost of production now has less to do with the variable expenses of producing each unit of output than with the sunk costs—research, product development, advertising—that a firm must incur before it turns out anything at all. The importance of subsidies that reduce those sunk costs, or that moderate the risks a firm runs in incurring them in advance of selling its product, is, therefore, much greater than before. Hence, such once-unexceptionable domestic policies as grants for worker training, reduced-rate government loans, and government-supported insurance now have international implications.

The amount of direct government spending on subsidies is significant. An estimated $39 billion was spent supporting farm prices in the United States, the European Community, and Japan in 1984, and the figure has risen sharply since then.[1] Capital-intensive industries in the United States are now lobbying for renewed subsidies in the form of accelerated depreciation, allowing them to write off investments more quickly against their federal income tax liabilities, while shipyards want the U.S. government to sponsor a new maritime construction program, and uranium mining companies would like Washington to promise to buy their output at a profitable price.

It has become fashionable to argue that where research-intensive, high-technology products are concerned, well-targeted government support can enhance a nation's welfare at the expense of other countries. Influenced by such thinking and by dire warnings about foreign companies conquering new technologies to the exclusion of U.S. firms, Congress has authorized cash subsidies for the development of superconducting materials, semiconductor manufacturing technology, and aircraft.

The reality, however, is that almost all of the national economic benefits from most types of supports disappear if other nations follow suit. If only one country subsidizes, its gains can be large; if several do so, the resulting waste of money in their unproductive effort to outsubsidize each other can only make them all poorer, not richer. Agreements under which countries jointly agree to desist from certain types of subsidies have the potential to check this flagrant misuse of resources.[2]

In principle, it should be possible to curb subsidies across the board. Doing so would require agreement on what types of measures should be prohibited and on which sorts of subsidies are permissible, and then proceeding in stages to reduce the level of those that are allowed. Negotiations along this line would be analogous to those in previous rounds of the GATT, in which countries first agreed to convert all of their protectionist trade barriers into tariffs and then sought agreement to reduce them gradually. One way of doing this would be to agree on a uniform method for calculating the extent of assistance each industry receives, including the negative impact of measures that raise the cost of an industry's inputs and thus harm its competitiveness.[3] If everyone were to establish a consensus on how subsidies are to be measured, then it would be relatively easy for all parties to concur in reducing them by a specific percentage.

An alternative approach would be for each country to list the foreign subsidy practices that it believes cause harm to its industries, and to state the specific foreign products against which it would impose countervailing duties if each of the subsidies is not eliminated. Timetables for changing or eliminating each individual subsidy would be negotiated among the countries directly concerned, turning the multilateral GATT negotiations over subsidies into an organized series of separate bilateral talks.[4]

In practice, however, the prospect of any sweeping agreement on subsidy practices is slim. In previous rounds of GATT negotiations, attempts to find broad definitions of allowable and illegal subsidies have gotten virtually nowhere. The number of possible measures and the variations among national practices are so great that a simple list of the permissible is not so simple to agree upon. In any case, many of the most frequently subsidized and supported industries enjoy sufficient political clout in their home countries to insist that they be treated as exceptions to whatever general rule is developed. Outlawing individual types of government assistance is likely to achieve little more than forcing government officials to design more ingenious subsidy programs. While a general framework for dealing with subsidies is worth striving for, any serious progress is likely to come only in discussions about individual industries. Agriculture, steel, textiles, and computer-related technology must be the high priorities because of pending domestic decisions and international agreements that must be renegotiated during the next four years.

An Agricultural Agenda

Subsidies are more ubiquitous in agriculture than in any other sector involved in international trade. At the same time, however, agricultural subsidies have been among the most intractable of international economic issues. Tariffs, the most visible and easily negotiable type of aid, are relatively unimportant in protecting farm-related industries. Instead, farmers benefit from a wide array of "domestic" programs that distort output, prices, and trade patterns. The average value of farm subsidies ranges from only 9 percent of the market value of domestic agricultural production in Australia to 72 percent in Japan.[5] Since the methods used to provide that income to farmers differ greatly from country to country, eliminating them by multilateral agreements has proven difficult.[6]

Their scope is astonishingly broad. In the nineteen major industrial countries, over half of all meat and dairy products are protected by quotas or other nontariff barriers. Wheat subsidies turned nine members of the European Community from net importers of 20 million tons of wheat annually in 1965 to net exporters of 10 million tons in 1983, while U.S. protection for sugar producers—and its effect in encouraging the use of nonsugar sweeteners—may soon cause sugar imports into the

United States to cease altogether. In developing countries, farmers often receive highly subsidized fertilizer, government assistance in mechanizing their farms, and low-interest credit, leading them to grow food in ways that may not be efficient. Farm aid programs generally do not come cheap. In the United States, each dollar of benefit to agricultural producers in 1985 cost taxpayers $1.38; a similar study of the Japanese economy in 1976 showed that each dollar of increased income for farmers cost $2.58.[7]

As part of the GATT negotiations, the United States proposed in 1987 to eliminate all agricultural subsidies within ten years. The suggestion was rightly derided as unrealistic, particularly given the tremendous growth in America's own farm subsidy spending during 1986 and 1987. The European Community, suffering from severe internal political disputes over agricultural policy, responded by urging a modest reduction in subsidies plus emergency measures to cut subsidy spending on a handful of key commodities. The third major force on agriculture within the GATT, the so-called "Cairns Group," headed by Australia, Canada, and Argentina, has been sharply critical of both the United States and the European Community, calling upon them to cut back on subsidies unilaterally.

To date the GATT negotiations on agricultural issues have achieved almost nothing. Indeed, the Reagan administration may have been far too sanguine about the prospects of a major agreement during the Uruguay Round. Yet international agricultural problems must be confronted quickly after the next president takes office. The basic legislation governing U.S. domestic agricultural policy must be reauthorized by Congress in 1990. If the basis of an international agreement has not been laid, Congress may make changes in U.S. farm programs that would make multilateral reductions in farm subsidies vastly more difficult to achieve.

In the current multilateral negotiations, the United States should adopt a far more modest and politically realistic goal than the total elimination of agricultural subsidies. The best approach would be to rely upon the concept of the "producer-subsidy equivalent," developed by the Organization of Economic Cooperation and Development, which quantifies the value of all programs and policies that lead to higher returns in agriculture. In the near term, the GATT could agree on exactly how the producer-subsidy equivalent is to be calculated, and could seek pledges from all members that they will not raise total subsidies affecting any crop above the current level. The second step could be a five-year reduction in the value of subsidies for each crop at a specified percentage each year, leaving further reductions and the ultimate elimination of trade-distorting subsidies to future negotiations.[8]

Even without an international agreement, there is much the new administration can do unilaterally to push for worldwide curbs on farm subsidies. The fact that American farmers are among the world's most efficient means that subsidies are not required to help them compete in international markets. The production subsidies U.S. farmers receive are merely elaborate methods of transferring income to the farm sector. As the Reagan administration has recognized, much the same objective could be achieved by decoupling farm support from production: rather than subsidizing farmers for each bushel of grain or gallon of milk, the government could provide income assistance through a program not linked to output. Programs that force consumers to subsidize farmers, such as regulation of milk prices and tariffs on imported beef, could be eliminated or scaled back in the same way. Individual farmers would have to produce as much or as little as they believed they could sell profitably on world markets. The likely result of decoupling would be a significant increase in U.S. farm output, driving down world prices and thereby raising the cost of production subsidies for those nations that persist in using them. That would surely increase the political pressure abroad for the international agreement.

In the past, unfortunately, the United States has often thrown its weight around in counterproductive ways when agricultural issues have been at stake. In 1983, in order to get rid of costly government-owned stocks of grain, the U.S. government paid farmers to take 77 million acres of land out of production. That effort did not enable American farmers to receive higher prices in the world market; instead, foreign producers increased their plantings nearly enough to make up for the U.S. production

the opening of the U.S. markets, were trying to sell shares in the British market."[2]

In principle, almost no one is opposed to greater international cooperation in financial market regulation. In practice, however, bringing international order out of the complex and diverse national rules that govern the actions of banks and securities traders is an arduous undertaking. Not only do different governments have disparate understandings of the problem, but major differences in financial market structures and legal systems from country to country make the establishment of consistent and equitable regulations a time-consuming process. Important first steps have been taken to bring banking rules into harmony, but the strong backing of the incoming U.S. administration will be required to help the process move forward as quickly as possible.

Several separate sets of issues are involved. In banking, the soundness of the world financial system is the fundamental concern, although trade-related issues, such as equal access for banks headquartered in one country to domestic markets in others, are also important. In the securities industry, the major points of negotiation have to do with protecting investors against fraud and market manipulation. In insurance, the right of companies from one country to receive equal treatment in foreign markets is most critical, along with limitations on regulations that hinder the introduction of new insurance products into foreign countries. And cutting across all three sectors are diverse national, and even state, regulations governing the structure of financial firms and the way in which they must conduct their various activities.

Harmonization or Uniformity?

Much of the limited progress to date in bringing financial regulatory systems into agreement can be attributed directly to financial disaster. The collapse of West Germany's Herstatt Bank in 1976 due to activities of its unsupervised Luxembourg subsidiary, and of Italy's Banco Ambrosiano in 1982 after fraudulent dealings by its subsidiaries in Luxembourg and Panama, pointed up the problems of leaving each country to oversee the banks located within its boundaries: each subsidiary reported to a different regulator, with no one responsible for appraising the soundness of the entire corporation. As a result, in 1983, regulators in Western Europe and North America agreed on the principle of consolidated supervision, giving a banking company's home country responsibility for supervising the entire organization, including subsidiaries abroad.

Regulatory cooperation in securities matters arose out of the need to share information pertaining to investigations of securities fraud and insider trading. Despite hesitations, regulators in all countries concurred that so much illicit activity crosses national borders that it cannot be policed from abroad, and, in the early 1980s, they began to sign formal accords to exchange otherwise confidential information for that purpose.

But the attainment of international agreements on financial regulation is complicated by the lack of a basic consensus about goals and purposes, as well as by the absence of the relatively clear economic definition of gains and losses that has made it possible to reach agreement on rules for trade in goods. Although the metaphor of a "level playing field" is on everyone's lips, financial companies face such different environments in each nation in which they compete—from differing tax systems and limits on diversification to disparate consumer protection laws and reporting requirements—that development of a single set of international standards governing finance is unlikely for years to come.

Nor is it clear that such an ambitious undertaking is worth the trouble, since the gains in terms of greater economic growth and more efficient global allocation of financial resources probably would be small. Therefore, rather than seeking a uniform set of financial regulations, it seems wiser to pursue the far more modest goal of harmonizing the most crucial regulations relating to safety and soundness. Countries have three basic incentives to work toward that end: to protect their own citizens who invest in foreign markets; to discourage other countries from competing in regulatory laxity to attract financial market business; and to prevent regulatory failures abroad that might drag their own economies into instability or even recession.

The United States took the lead in achieving the first major step in this direction, which was the July 1988 agreement on minimum capital standards for banks among the United States, Canada, Japan, and nine European countries. Its experience in that remarkable negotiation illustrates the difficulties of seeking international accord on the novel issues involved with financial market regulation.

The leading banking countries have widely differing banking traditions. In Germany, banks are major and active shareholders in commercial enterprises, from construction companies to auto manufacturers; in the United States, banking and commerce are separated by law. Banks in Japan base their lending decisions, in part, on administrative guidance from their government, while major parts of the French banking system are still owned by the government. Swiss banks may engage freely in investment banking, while British banks may do so only through separate subsidiaries. Yet, despite these differences, twelve major banking nations, including Sweden, Switzerland, as well as most members of the European Community, felt it imperative to seek agreement on the basic definition of bank capital, the funds banks maintain to meet claims and cover their losses.

Several factors led to the conclusion that international rules were needed. One was equity: as banks spread across national boundaries, those based in countries with less-restrictive capital requirements, including Japan, have an unfair advantage over those from countries that require banks to keep more capital on hand to back up their loans. An international standard for how much capital a bank must maintain should eliminate that distortion. A second concern was over potential claims of regulatory discrimination. Some countries define bank capital differently from others, at times causing foreign regulators to question applications to engage in new activities when regulators in the home countries see no problem.

A third worry was that the close interrelationships among banks in different countries could cause a failure in one country to trigger failures in others. The knowledge that banks active in one country meet reasonable standards of safety and soundness in another could help bank regulators sleep better at night. The fourth major question, which had been the subject of considerable domestic debate in the United States long before the international agreement, was how to deal with the many nonlending activities in which major banks now engage, from interest rate swaps to lines of credit. Banks in the United States have not been required to maintain capital reserves against such transactions to protect them against potential losses, as they must with traditional loans. Complicating matters further is the fact that many bank assets now take the form, not of individual loans, but of securities consisting of a package of loans purchased from another lender whose enforcement of quality standards is difficult to assure. Reaching international agreement on capital standards would accomplish little unless these new types of bank risks were addressed.[3]

The issue of creating similar capital standards throughout the industrialized world first came up in the 1970s at the Bank for International Settlements, an institution in Basel, Switzerland, often described as "the central bankers' bank." Although the United States does not belong to the organization, it has participated informally in discussions about bank capital in recent years. But the search for a uniform standard floundered due to the diversity of the various nations' separate regulatory schemes. An approach that seemed right for regulators in the United States, whose greatest concern was the risks of nontraditional banking activity, seemed wrong for West Germany, where bank reserves play a direct role in managing the money supply; for Japan, where regulators do not require as much shareholder investment as is common in other countries; and for the United Kingdom, which saw a risk that if it adopted stronger requirements, foreign banks would find London a less-attractive location.

It took unified action by the United States and Britain to force the matter. With talks at the Bank for International Settlements at a standstill, U.S. and British authorities worked out an agreement in February 1987 establishing uniform capital standards for banks from one country operating in the other. The other leading countries, fearing the bilateral agreement could work to their disadvantage, quickly fell into line. A proposed set of international principles for regulation of bank capital was announced in December 1987, establishing stiff rules for the amount of capital banks must maintain, defining how much shareholder equity is required, and specifying what other resources may constitute "capital." The rules, which were approved in final form in July 1988, lay out how much capital must be used to back various nonlending activities according to a uniform understanding of the risks each activity entails.

Despite general approval for the concept of uniform standards, the banking industry's reaction to the specific proposals illustrates the practical difficulty of bringing national regulatory systems into closer harmony. Bankers in the United States claimed that the guidelines blurred the difference between banks and bank holding companies, a point unimportant in Europe but significant in America; that their treatment of some accounting issues peculiar to the United States will make expansion more difficult; and that the proposal wrongly assesses the relative riskiness of various endeavors.[4]

The greatest concern, however, was that any effort to increase capital requirements for banks, even on an international basis, could work to the benefit of other types of financial institutions. Banks' costs will rise, while those of investment banks, insurance companies, and other competitors in the business of lending money will not. "The principle is unassailable: more consistent capital requirements help level the global playing field," admitted Willard C. Butcher, chairman of Chase Manhattan Corporation, the third-largest banking company in the United States. But, he worried, "If, as proposed, capital requirements for most banks around the world are raised, are we driving more business away from the banks?"[5]

Capital standards, complex as they are, may turn out to be one of the easier subjects on which to reach international banking agreements. If the risks of instability in world financial markets are to be reduced significantly, regulations in other areas—standards for determining when loans should be declared nonperforming and how banks should then handle them, bank taxation, clearing of banking and securities transactions, deposit insurance—must also be brought into harmony. This harmonization will have widespread effects beyond the banking industry, determining such things as banks' willingness to extend international loans and the degree to which corporate financing is done by or outside the banking system. Bank regulators have a full negotiating agenda for decades to come, one that is certain to become more intensely political as the import of the issue becomes more clearly understood.

Regulating the Markets

Modest as the results of international cooperation in banking regulation may appear to date, bank regulators are miles ahead of their counterparts who must deal with the securities markets. International harmonization of securities regulation is an idea that badly needs a push from government leaders if it is to overcome formidable political and economic obstacles.

Clearly, the stock, bond, and futures markets are becoming more international by the day. Sales of bonds outside the issuer's own country soared from $38 billion in 1980 to $254 billion in 1986 and $228 billion in 1987, making international bond sales a more important source of corporate finance than international bank lending. U.S. companies raised $45 billion in the international bond market in 1987. Cross-border equity trading more than doubled in that year, from $750 billion to $1.5 trillion,[6] of which $482 billion was bought and sold on the stock exchanges in New York. Private sector pension funds in the United States hold $45 billion in foreign securities. And, individual U.S. investors are involved as well: in 1986, foreign companies raised $2.3 billion in public stock offerings on U.S. exchanges.[7]

At present, however, countries regulate their own securities markets, and they do so in very different manners. Trading rules, accounting standards, mandatory disclosures, and other investor protections vary greatly from one market to another. This complicates the business of securities issuance, particularly for larger corporations, and exposes investors to uncertain risks if they venture into instruments registered in another country. According to a private estimate by one U.S. bank, up to 30 percent of all foreign securities transactions do not clear. Although buyer and seller have agreed on a price, cash and stock never change hands.

The divergence in regulations can disadvantage American investors. One foreign company tendering for the shares of another foreign company, for example, may face unwanted disclosure requirements if U.S. shareholders are involved; to avoid U.S. regulations, the company may declare that American citizens are ineligible for its tender offer, or may offer them only cash when shareholders in other countries have a choice of cash or stock.[8] Lax foreign regulation may also abet illegal activities, such as insider trading, in U.S. markets. In 1986 and 1987, more than one-third of the cases of suspected insider stock trading that U.S. exchanges asked the Securities and Exchange Commission to investigate involved foreign brokerage firms.[9]

What little international cooperation exists in regulating the securities markets is largely the result of the efforts by the Securities and Exchange Commission to attack insider trading. The Commission has negotiated memoranda of understanding with regulators in Britain, Switzerland, Japan, and Canada to share information when a suspect is alleged to have engaged in illegal trades based on knowledge of important nonpublic information about the company whose shares are being traded. These agreements have encouraged foreign countries to make available information about specific trades and bank accounts needed to prosecute criminal cases in the United States. Where no agreements exist, investigating insider trading is difficult; the federal authorities routinely ignore suspected insider trading emanating from Panama, Luxembourg, Liechtenstein, and other countries because of the difficulty of obtaining information. Even where an accord exists, the record of success in obtaining cooperation is spotty, in good part because authorities in such financially important nations as Switzerland and Japan regard insider trading as a far less serious matter than do those in the United States.[10]

By contrast, there are no international agreements at all on the critical issue of short sales, the advance sale of stock the seller does not yet own. Short sales, which often require sellers to borrow stock from their brokers, are regulated in the United States but not in Great Britain.

Margin requirements, which regulate the degree to which a securities transaction can be financed by money borrowed from the broker, are another contentious issue. Margin requirements are among the strongest tools regulators possess to restrain markets' natural tendency to speculative excess. Extremely low margin requirements—allowing investors to enter the market with little money down—create a risk that if a sudden decline in prices reduces the value of the shares brokers hold as collateral, then forced sales to raise cash to repay margin loans could send markets into a tailspin, possibly causing a sharp economic contraction. U.S. regulators have attempted to limit the risks by requiring investors to put as much as 50 percent down when buying stock, creating an incentive for foreign stock markets to impose less-stringent requirements to attract customers. As more and more companies list their shares on exchanges in several different countries, this could become an important factor in determining where transactions occur, with competitive pressure interfering with prudent regulation.

International competition has also hindered efforts to have government regulators set margin rules for U.S. futures markets, as some experts have recommended in the wake of the 1987 crash. At present, the Federal Reserve allows futures exchanges to establish their own margin requirements for each type of futures contract; as a result, the average down payment required to invest in futures is only about 15 percent, far less than that for stocks. Domestically, of course, the battle over margin rules is part of the ongoing competition between New York's stock exchanges and Chicago's futures markets. There is also a legitimate concern, however, that imposing significantly higher margins on futures trading in the United States alone could simply encourage U.S. investors to trade futures in foreign markets, an undertaking made relatively easy by the widespread use of computers.[11]

The list of policies in need of international harmonization in this area is daunting: procedures for clearing and settlement of a securities purchase or sale; pre-arranged responses, if any, to sudden marketwide price collapses;[12] registration and assurance of the financial integrity of brokers and dealers; and the methods used by exchanges to disclose prices and offers. David S. Ruder, chairman of the Securities and Exchange Commission, has suggested the development of minimum disclosure standards for stock and bond issuers as the top international priority,[13] but, despite widespread agreement in principle, harmonizing national regulations will be extremely difficult. Uniform disclosure requires uniform international accounting rules and auditing standards, an issue so complex that not even the European Community's effort to create a single European financial market has dared address it.

Moreover, some issues concerning international securities trading are not susceptible to government regulation at all. The free market, for example, may be better at forcing agreement on rules for clearing trades than are regulators; those stock exchanges that do not assure that trades are completed quickly and accurately will lose business to those that do. Rather than setting detailed rules, regulators might seek to agree only on basic principles, such as the maximum time within which transactions must clear, and leave the details to the private sector.

Insurance Issues

Of all the fields of financial services, discussion of harmonizing regulations is least advanced in insurance. While the failure of a major insurance company has the potential to create the same type of cascading financial collapse as the closing of a bank or the widespread sale of a fraudulent security, the differences between insurance and other financial services are substantial. The extensive use of private reinsurance markets to spread risk widely means that each insurance company has occasion to carefully scrutinize the stability of others with which it does business, providing some degree of market discipline. At the same time, the receipt of insurance payments to cover losses rarely makes the difference between life and death for a large corporation; the analogy of a bank failure wiping out its major customers rarely applies. As a result, one nation's regulatory laxity in insurance offers far less reason for other countries to be concerned than is the case in banking or securities.

The international issue in insurance is not one of safety and soundness, but of trade. Many nations maintain restrictions that put foreign-owned insurance companies at a disadvantage or bar them altogether. These barriers, which are among the many subjects under discussion at the General Agreement on Tariffs and Trade's negotiations on services trade, have become a burning issue for expansion-minded U.S. insurance companies, which found themselves unable to enter South Korea, Taiwan, and other countries until the U.S. government threatened trade retaliation. Matters such as the right of one country's insurance companies to establish subsidiaries in another, the right to face regulatory restraints no greater than those applied to domestic firms, the right to offer new products that meet general regulatory standards, and the right of customers to buy insurance from whatever firm they prefer are all major points of discussion. Although many foreign insurance companies have American subsidiaries, the United States is not exempt from charges of protectionism: until 1988, for example, merchant ships subsidized by the U.S. government could be insured only by American-owned marine insurance companies.

Despite the great interest of American insurers in lowering barriers abroad, the new administration will have a difficult time in international negotiations. The reason is that it lacks the authority to negotiate on insurance matters.

Under the McCarran-Ferguson Act of 1945, insurance regulation is the responsibility of state rather than federal authorities. The difficulty this poses for federal efforts to open foreign insurance markets became apparent in 1988, when B.A.T. Industries, a British firm, made an undesired offer to buy Farmers Group, a California-based insurer. To complete the transaction, B.A.T. needed regulatory approval in each of the nine states in which Farmers maintained a subsidiary. Several states rejected B.A.T.'s application, among them California, where the insurance commissioner found that the small quantity of B.A.T. shares owned by various foreign governments and government pension funds made the company ineligible to engage in the insurance business under state law. Although foreign countries may find such a regulation objectionable, only California authorities, not federal authorities, have the power to change it.

Keeping the McCarran-Ferguson Act, which also grants insurers a limited exemption from antitrust law allowing them jointly to set rates, analyze risks, and design policy forms, has long been the insurance industry's foremost political goal. However, it will be difficult for the new administration to take the lead in liberalizing the world insurance market as long as the law remains in place. Even if political realities preclude shifting regulation of the insurance industry from state to federal control, Congress should amend the law to give federal commitments to lower barriers to international insurance trade precedence over state laws and rules to the contrary.

The Global Financial Challenge

The pending unification of the West European economy, scheduled for 1992, makes it necessary for the United States to find ways to promote international cooperation in financial market regulation as quickly as possible. At the same time, it offers a unique opportunity to do so.

Until 1987, Europe's financial markets were generally highly regulated and conservative; while European banks have long ranked among the world's largest, securities markets have been small and illiquid. "Big Bang," the 1987 deregulation of retail securities trading in Britain, was a major step toward changing that reputation. Other countries were forced to loosen regulatory strings to compete with London. France deregulated the stodgy Paris Bourse in 1988 and created a new financial futures market, Italy encouraged greater trading in Milan, and West Germany's small regional stock exchanges discussed unification into a larger, more liquid institution.

In February 1988, the Commission of the European Communities, the administrative arm of the twelve-member organization, took a major step to transform the banking and securities industries across the continent. After years of discussions on banking, the Community's members concluded that, in the words of one official, "[T]he meticulous harmonization efforts in the banking field, judged by their results—have proven to be impractical and cumbersome in many respects."[14] They tried a new approach, issuing a banking directive that abolishes the need for a bank to obtain a separate license in each country. Instead, a bank based in any Community country will be able to operate in all other member countries according to the rules of its home country, an arrangement that is expected to encourage each country to liberalize its banking regulations in order to help its banks compete abroad.[15] The European banking license will include the right to engage in securities trading, portfolio management, and underwriting, thereby setting the stage for the transformation of Europe's major banks into diversified international financial service companies serving a market of 320 million people. Initially, all of the national financial regulatory agencies within Europe will remain in place. As regulatory distinctions among member countries fade, however, support for a single Community-wide regulatory system is sure to grow.

Even as Europe is significantly reshaping its system of financial regulation, the other nations that are home to important financial centers, Canada and Japan, are also in the midst of encouraging more competition in financial markets. While old regulatory systems are in flux and the momentum for deregulation remains strong, there is a propitious opportunity to seek international agreement on more harmonious rules. Once the markets have adjusted to their new freedom and new regulations have entered force, particularly in Europe, it will be more difficult to persuade both national officials and firms in the financial industry that additional steps to harmonize regulations are desirable.

Unfortunately, the United States is in a poor position to initiate negotiations because of its inability to reach any sort of domestic consensus on financial regulatory issues. Congress has spent years discussing reform of the Glass-Steagall Act, which separates commercial banking and investment banking into two quite distinct sectors, without successfully redefining what the relationship between banking and securities operations should be. In addition, proposals to make U.S. regulation of securities trading and futures trading more consistent—the two types of markets are now regulated by totally separate agencies, which are overseen by separate congressional committees and apply fundamentally different regulatory approaches—have not received serious discussion, despite recommendations made in the wake of the stock market crash. And, in response to the boom in hostile corporate takeovers since 1983, numerous states have established new laws concerning tender offers and corporate governance, increasing the regulatory diversity within the United States and making it even more difficult for the U.S. government to negotiate such matters on an international plane.

International forces will compel the United States to confront its own regulatory restrictions. European Community officials have made clear that access to Western Europe's banking market after 1992 will be strictly on a reciprocal basis: European subsidiaries of American banks will not be given free rein to trade or underwrite securities within the Community unless the United States extends that same privilege to European banks. Canadian authorities, too, have raised objections to U.S. banks' entering Canada's securities industry while Canadian institutions cannot do the same in the United States. And the use of state securities and insurance laws to attack foreign-owned companies is certain to occasion increasing protest from abroad. If the next administration and Congress cannot cut the Gordian knot that has for years blocked action on these issues, U.S. firms may find themselves frozen out of foreign markets, and American trade negotiators may lose their leverage at the bargaining table.

The next U.S. administration should surely encourage efforts to bring banking and securities regulations into line around the world. As the former chief economist of the New York Stock Exchange has noted, "It is just at moments when the economic policymakers are having trouble getting things right when the professionals who are in charge of regulatory and self-regulatory bodies have a singular public mission and responsibility for helping to assure that instability in markets is contained, no matter how inhospitable the economic climate."[16] Although the issues are too technical for detailed presidential involvement, public support and high-level staff interest will encourage governments abroad to make regulatory harmonization a higher priority, and will strengthen the negotiating position of U.S. regulators in the face of the industries they regulate.

The most substantial steps the new administration can take to help level the worldwide financial playing field, however, are domestic. Not until Congress and the administration both agree to break down the walls separating the banking and securities industries, and make it clear that securities regulation is a federal responsibility, will the United States be in a position to lead the campaign for international agreement on regulations.

Notes

1. E. Gerald Corrigan, *Financial Market Structure: A Longer View* (New York: Federal Reserve Bank of New York, 1987), p. 16.
2. Nicholas deB. Katzenbach, *An Overview of Program Trading and Its Impact on Current Market Prices* (New York: New York Stock Exchange, 1987), p. 20.
3. Jeffrey C. Marquardt, "Interactions among Countries in Financial Supervision: A U.S. Perspective" (Paper presented to the annual meeting of the American Economic Association, Chicago, Ill., December 1987, mimeographed).
4. American Bankers Association comments to Federal Reserve Board on risk-based capital guidelines, May 13, 1988. Also see George Melloan, "Global Bank Regulation Fans a New Debate," *Wall Street Journal*, March 15, 1988, p. 35.
5. Willard C. Butcher, remarks to World Paper Conference, Boston, Mass., April 14, 1988.
6. E. Gerald Corrigan, address to Group of Thirty Symposium on Clearance and Settlement Issues in the Global Securities Markets, London, March 9, 1988.
7. U.S. Securities and Exchange Commission, *Report of the Staff of the U.S. Securities and Exchange Commission to the Senate Committee on Banking, Housing and Urban Affairs and the House Committee on Energy and Commerce on the Internationalization of the Securities Markets* (Washington, D.C.: Securities and Exchange Commission, 1987), pp. 1–4, 11–12.
8. Ibid, pp. 111–298.
9. Thomas E. Ricks, "Foreign Brokerages Appear Frequently in Insider-Trading Reports, Study Says," *Wall Street Journal*, June 6, 1988, p. 3.
10. A. E. Cullison, "Latest Threat from the West," *Journal of Commerce*, July 29, 1987, p. 14A; Thomas E. Ricks, "House Aides Fault SEC, Big Board on Foreign Insider-Trade Inquiries," *Wall Street Journal*, June 7, 1988, p. 3.
11. Nathaniel C. Nash, "Fed Chief against Rise in Index-future Margins," *New York Times*, June 15, 1988, p. D6.
12. Edward J. Markey, "Give the Markets Regulatory Cohesion," *The International Economy*, vol. 2, no. 3 (May/June 1988), pp. 19–21.
13. David S. Ruder, "Regulation of International Securities Markets," speech to the American Stock Exchange Conference, Washington, D.C., October 19, 1987.
14. Georgios Zavvos, "EC Strategy for the Banking Sector: The Perspective of 1992," *European Affairs* (Spring 1988), p. 102.

15. Commission of the European Communities, "Proposal for a Second Council Directive on the coordination of laws, regulations and administrative provisions related to the taking-up and pursuit of the business of credit institutions and amending Directive 77/780/EEC," February 16, 1988.

16. Roger Kubarych, "International Harmonization: The Economic and Financial Environment" (New York: New York Stock Exchange, 1988, mimeographed).

9

Who Owns America?

"The Coming Foreign Raiders;" "Foreign Firms Build More U.S. Factories, Vex American Rivals;" and "Japanese Takeover Artists Are Learning Fast."[1] The headlines bespeak a deepseated fear that foreigners are coming to control major portions of the U.S. economy. In the first half of 1988 alone, such all-American companies as Federated Department Stores, Firestone Tire and Rubber, and Koppers Company passed into foreign hands, raising concerns that America is losing command of its own industrial base. So many Japanese are buying houses in Honolulu that the city's mayor called for a ban on foreign ownership of residential property, claiming it is "not fair to Americans."[2]

The public clamor for action is loud enough that legislation requiring all foreign investors to register with the U.S. government passed the House of Representatives in 1987, and a provision authorizing the president to block individual foreign investments on national security grounds nearly won congressional approval in 1988. Influential voices in the media and in business have called for limitations on foreign ownership of U.S. companies. In February 1988, even the U.S. Trade Representative saw fit to warn his foreign colleagues of an American backlash against foreign investors.[3]

This fear of foreign domination is likely to be a major feature of the next presidential term, because the flow of foreign money into U.S. companies is nowhere near its peak. Although there are a number of reasons foreigners might want to own a share of the United States—corporate strategy, an enormous internal market offering large economies of scale, the low risk of expropriation or political instability, a hedge against trade protectionism—the chronic U.S. current account deficits are the major factors driving new foreign direct investment. Large U.S. trade deficits are likely to continue into the early 1990s, leaving foreigners with fistfuls of dollars not required for the purchase of goods or services. Somehow or other, unless it is exchanged for marks or pounds or yen at an unattractive rate of exchange, that money must be invested. As long as that is the case, rapid growth in foreign investment is likely to continue.

However, it is not the magnitude of foreign investment that worries many Americans as much as it is the types of investments that are made. There were few protests when foreign ownership of U.S. corporate bonds doubled from 1982 to 1986. No objections were raised as foreign ownership of corporate stock increased 160 percent over the same period, leaving foreigners holding more than one in twenty shares on the New York Stock Exchange. It is the increase in foreign *direct* investment, defined as more than 10 percent ownership of a property in the United States, that leads to the anguished claim that America is surrendering control of its economy to foreigners.

There are, in fact, legitimate reasons for the new administration to study restrictions on foreign investment in the United States. Restrictions on foreign investment may serve narrow purposes of national security, and they may be effective in pushing other countries to lower their barriers to Americans who might wish to invest abroad. But neither of these issues lies at the crux of the emotional debate over foreign investment today, a debate the next president will have to struggle constantly to defuse.

The popular concern over foreign direct investment stems from a fear that foreigners will be able to use their control of property and business enterprises to the disadvantage of American citizens. One frequent objection is that as American firms are taken over by foreigners, the new owners will be able to exercise monopoly power over the U.S. market. Another is that foreign owners will be able to take the technology developed by American firms and put it to work for the benefit of their own country. A third, rather ironic in view of the enormous dislocations caused by the restructuring of U.S. manufacturing over the past six years, is that foreign owners will close facilities in the United States and "export" the jobs to their home countries, or will maintain U.S. plants as marginal operations with outmoded technology. A fourth is that foreign corporations in the United States are more likely to procure services and components from their home countries rather than locally. A fifth is that by providing employment in American communities, foreigners will come to have a powerful voice in the making of national economic policy—a prospect vividly illustrated in the fall of 1987, when thousands of U.S. employees of Japan's Toshiba Corporation as well as city and state politicians protested congressional legislation punishing Toshiba for selling technologically sophisticated milling machines to the Soviet Union.[4]

These fears, however, have little in common with the facts. Foreign-owned firms in the United States are rarely in a position to exert monopoly power; the industries in which foreign investment has been most significant during the 1980s tend not to be dominated by a small number of large firms. Nor is there evidence that foreign investors have deprived Americans of the fruits of their own research. While most foreign direct investors—Canadians are an exception—prefer industries with high research and-development expenditures, that fact suggests only that foreign investors, like American investors, have avoided declining industries in which little research is undertaken.[5] This should come as no surprise, since American-based multinational corporations with direct investments abroad also have a relatively heavy involvement in research and development.[6] As is the case with many U.S.–based firms, large foreign companies are increasingly doing research around the globe in order to obtain access to the best scientific talent available.

Fears that jobs will be exported notwithstanding, foreign investors are unlikely to purchase facilities in the United States for the purpose of closing them down. Although some foreign companies may put their newest machinery to work in their home market first and transfer technology only with delay, many others, in industries such as chemicals and medical technology, operate on the technological forefront in the United States.

The U.S. subsidiary of a foreign corporation is likely to turn out products similar to those of its parent company, suggesting that foreign direct investors see the purchase of production capacity in the United States as a way to expand their activities in the U.S. market. Foreign owners, with new production methods, marketing approaches, and an ability to achieve economies of scale that smaller U.S.–owned firms may lack, have given obsolescent plants in the tire, automotive, electronics, and chemical industries new life. In many cases, the alternative to foreign acquisition is not U.S. ownership, but rather withdrawal from key markets or even the shutdown of a company that is not able to compete on the global scale required in many industries today.

There are other gains from foreign direct investment as well. The fact that a foreign company purchases assets in the United States indicates that it was the highest bidder; the Americans who sell their shares and real estate, including the funds that hold most workers' retirement pensions, collect the greatest possible capital gains. And foreign direct investment often brings an additional benefit to all consumers in the form of increased competition. Far from monopolizing sectors of industry, foreign firms entering the U.S. market have increased the number of strong companies active in such industries as auto manufacturing and steel production, bringing about lower prices. Perhaps the only negative effect of foreign direct investment in manufacturing is that foreign companies have a relatively strong propensity to import. American affiliates of foreign companies imported two and a half times as much as they exported in 1986.[7] U.S.–based multinationals, in contrast, export more from the United States than they import.[8] But those ratios of imports to exports are likely to converge as foreign-owned factories in the United States develop more domestic sources for components and as factories owned by U.S.–based firms increasingly rely on components from abroad.

Despite the salutary effects of foreign direct investment, the sight of a familiar U.S. corporate name caught in the embrace of a foreign giant raises highly nationalistic feelings in a country which has grown accustomed to hearing politicians, corporate chiefs, and union leaders blame foreigners for domestic economic woes.[9] Because of the degree of concern foreign investment in the U.S. economy continues to attract, the issue is certain to simmer throughout the next president's administration, ready to erupt at any political opportunity.

The Other Side of the Coin

It is often forgotten that foreign direct investment in the United States is only one side of the coin. Americans have an enormous number of investments abroad, and those investments are growing at a rapid rate. Although the accuracy of the government's statistics both on domestic investment by foreigners and on foreign investment by U.S. firms is open to question, the long-term trends in both cases are clear. In 1987, even as foreigners' direct investments in the United States increased by $42 billion, Americans' direct investments in other countries grew by $49 billion. The total amount of direct U.S. investment abroad was $309 billion at the end of 1987, far higher than the $262 billion of foreign direct investment in the United States. Because all of these investments are listed at book value in official statistics, the fact that U.S. investments abroad are, on average, older than foreign direct investments in the United States means that American investments abroad are understated relative to foreign investment.

The amount of U.S. direct investment abroad more than tripled between 1973 and 1987. In addition, as foreign securities markets have become more liquid, American holdings of non-controlling positions in foreign corporate stock have increased at a faster rate than foreign ownership of American shares since 1982.

There is more than a little irony in the fact that Americans are so worried about others' investing in their economy when American-owned firms, among the first to undertake investments abroad, have long controlled critical industries in other countries. Starting in 1904, for example, American firms developed Chile's copper mining industry, its main source of foreign exchange; they were responsible for the country's entire output of copper as late as 1967. During the early 1960s, in Peru, notes one scholar, "Most of [the] major commodities—cotton, sugar, fish products, lead, zinc, silver, copper, and the bulk of its oil— were produced and/or exported by American-owned companies."[10] Such investments continue apace, as U.S.–based firms seek to serve foreign markets from local plants.[11] U.S.–based Ford Motor Company and General Motors Corporation are the second- and third-largest producers of automobiles in Britain. Even as foreign chemical companies acquired 121 chemical-related businesses in the United States in 1985, U.S.–based chemical firms made eighty-three purchases abroad.[12]

The U.S. government has long been at pains to convince others that American direct investment in their economies is harmless and even beneficial. Historically, the United States has acted firmly to protect the interests of American-owned companies with assets in foreign countries, even to the point of destabilizing governments that attempted to limit direct investment by U.S. firms. Since the enormous foreign debts of developing countries began to drag down these economies in 1982, the United States has advocated that debtor nations accept more foreign direct investment and allow creditors to swap debt for equity in local companies in return for assistance in refinancing or rescheduling their loans. The Reagan administration encouraged developing countries to reduce their debt burdens by allowing foreign-held debt to be swapped for equity in domestic companies, turning it from passively held assets into direct foreign investments—a strategy not dissimilar to the one many foreign creditors have been pursuing in the United States. Reducing Canada's restrictions on foreign investment has been an important goal in bilateral relations, and Canadian agreement to further reduce barriers to direct investment represented a concession to the United States during the negotiation of the 1987 U.S.–Canada free trade agreement.

Nor has foreign investment traditionally been an emotional subject in the United States. Ever since British capital helped build American canals and railroads in the nineteenth century, the United States has been relatively open to foreign investors. Aside from the expropriation of holdings of German-owned companies during World War I and World War II and passage of the Agriculture Foreign Investment Disclosure Act, which requires foreign owners of farmland to report their holdings to the U.S. Department of Agriculture, in the 1970s, there have been few restrictions on foreign investment activity. As late as 1983, Congress repealed a law requiring foreign owners of real property to list their holdings with the Internal Revenue Service lest it discourage foreigners from bringing their money to the United States without the knowledge of their home governments.

The United States imposes far fewer limits on investment by foreign citizens and corporations than any other industrial country. At present, foreigners are barred from a relative handful of industries; they may not hold U.S. broadcast licenses, own U.S.–flag ships, control oil pipelines, or possess more than 25 percent of the shares of a U.S. airline. Even these exceptions can be evaded, as the Australian publisher Rupert Murdoch discovered in 1985 when he quickly acquired U.S. citizenship in order to obtain permission to purchase a group of television stations. Aside from these and a few other relatively minor investment restrictions aimed at foreigners, U.S. law provides only for government review of foreign acquisition of companies with defense-related activities, and no proposed transaction has ever been blocked under that provision. Stated U.S. policy in bilateral and multilateral talks has been to get other countries to remove their barriers, not to raise its own.

The Foreign Takeover "Wave"

The oft-reported claim that foreign direct investment in the United States is at record levels is true, but it is earth-shattering only in the absence of historical perspective. Foreign direct investment in the United States has set a new record every year for decades, climbing steadily from $13.9 billion in 1971 to $262 billion at the end of 1987. The rate of increase in the stock of foreign-owned assets, aside from such purely financial assets as corporate bonds and U.S. Treasury bills, is not particularly startling. Although the value of foreign direct investment jumped $42 billion in 1987 from $220 billion at the end of 1986, that 19 percent growth is by no means a record. The total amount of foreign direct investment grew at a faster rate in 1973, 1974, 1978, 1979, 1980, 1981, 1984, and 1986. If there is a "wave" of foreign investment sweeping the United States, it started long ago.[13] In fact, the proportion of all incoming foreign money taking the form of direct investment, as opposed to passive investment in financial instruments, hit its peak back in 1981.

The total number of foreign investments, including the number of American companies acquired by foreigners, has actually declined in recent years; according to preliminary figures, the number of investments in 1987, 557, was less than half that reported in 1981.[14] In some areas, foreign investment interest has long since peaked: in 1987, the amount of farmland in foreign hands increased less than 2 percent, a far cry from the growth rates of a decade earlier.

Nor is it the case that foreign investors are zeroing in on the U.S. manufacturing sector. Barely one-third of foreign investment in the United States is in manufacturing; the proportion was lower in 1987 than it was in 1982.[15] The number of Americans working for foreign-owned manufacturers, which grew by an average of 45,000 a year from 1981 to 1985, actually fell in 1986 and accounts for about 6 percent of all manufacturing workers. Throughout the entire economy, roughly 3 million workers, out of a workforce exceeding 120 million, are in the employ of foreign concerns.[16] The book value of foreign-owned property, plants and equipment used in manufacturing was $111 billion in 1985; although the figures are not precisely comparable, the total value of the nation's manufacturing equipment and structures that year was $1.5 trillion, suggesting that foreigners controlled roughly 7 percent of the nation's manufacturing assets. In some sectors, however, the proportion is significantly higher. In chemicals, for instance, where large foreign firms have maintained a U.S. presence for decades, experts estimate that 25 percent to 30 percent of productive assets in the United States are foreign owned.

What has caused alarm in the United States is not so much the extent of foreign ownership of American assets but rather who those foreign owners are. In particular, Japanese companies, slower than their European and Canadian counterparts to invest abroad, have bid aggressively for control of U.S. companies. Japanese foreign direct investment in the United States increased from less than $10 billion at the end of 1982 to over $33 billion in December 1987, giving Japan the third-largest foreign direct investment position in the United States, behind the United Kingdom and the Netherlands. That development, however, is of less consequence than it may at first appear. Nearly half of that Japanese investment is in wholesale trade, such as U.S. distribution systems of Japanese automakers and electronics companies. Japanese companies held only $5 billion in direct investment in U.S. manufacturing at the end of 1987, less than two-thirds as much as that held by companies based in Switzerland.[17] Between 1979 and 1985, only 12 percent of all foreign investment in U.S. manufacturing came from Japan.

One reason for the special concern about Japanese manufacturing investment is that Japanese companies, by and large, operate differently from the companies to which Americans are accustomed. Unlike most major transnational corporations based in North America and Europe, Japanese manufacturers have tended not to treat their foreign subsidiaries as part of an integrated global manufacturing operation. Instead, they have generally kept research and development work and the manufacture of high-value-added components in Japan, using their foreign subsidiaries only for final assembly, marketing, and distribution. For the United States, this has meant that Japanese subsidiaries import both components and technology to a greater extent than other foreign-owned companies do. The rapid rise in the relative cost of doing business in Japan, however, is forcing many Japanese companies to move more of their operations overseas, and will likely cause Japanese multinationals to behave more like German- or Canadian-based multinationals in the future.

In banking, another sector about which nationalistic concerns run strong, the number of Japanese-owned banking operations increased from fifty-nine a decade ago to ninety-eight in 1987.

This increase, however, has paralleled the general growth of international banking. The proportion of Japanese banks among all foreign-controlled financial institutions in the United States actually fell from 21.9 percent in 1978 to 14.9 percent in 1987, indicating that other foreign investors are expanding their banking activities in the United States even more quickly.[18]

Despite the intense publicity given to Japanese ventures, they are not particularly large; only two of the fifty largest direct investment transactions from 1979 to 1985 involved Japanese firms. In general, Japanese investors in the United States seem to be motivated by many of the same factors driving direct investment by companies and individuals in other nations, although they are more likely to invest in large plants with relatively labor-intensive production processes. The comparatively strong growth of the U.S. economy since 1982 has been a major factor prompting Japanese investment. On the other hand, U.S. trade barriers against imports seem not to be related to the pattern of Japanese direct investment, although restraints on auto imports are a clear exception.[19]

The impression that a massive fire sale of U.S. assets is underway, then, is seriously mistaken. Instead, two other trends are at work. First, private foreign investors chose during 1987 to reduce the proportion of their portfolios consisting of U.S. bonds, particularly Treasury securities, and to shift that money into assets that might protect them against the continuing depreciation of the dollar. Second, foreign corporations, which have been slower than their U.S. counterparts to operate on a global scale, are finally taking the plunge. In particular, Japanese manufacturers are busily setting up plants in Europe, Brazil, Mexico, and Southeast Asia. Their investment in the United States is simply one manifestation of this larger trend.

Security and Reciprocity

What would happen if the U.S. government suddenly said, "Stop!" The answer is speculative, but the probable result of a ban on foreign direct investment would be a sharp drop in foreign willingness to lend America money. After all, much of the attraction the United States offers foreign capital is the depth of its capital markets: investors can move easily between commercial paper, corporate bonds, government securities, corporate equities, and direct investments as their changing needs and their assessment of risks might dictate. Restricting those options would give international investors reason to prefer other countries. U.S. interest rates would have to rise in order to draw in the needed foreign capital, or the dollar would have to fall, or, if capital flight were great enough, both events could well occur simultaneously. Since the U.S. government is certain to be the high bidder for whatever capital it needs to fund its budget deficit, private borrowers, including companies looking to build new facilities and buy new equipment, would find it more difficult to obtain the capital they need. The effects of a reduction in the flow of foreign funds to the United States would be serious: in five of the last eight years, more than 20 percent of the corporate bonds issued in the United States have been purchased by foreigners.[20]

Many U.S. companies would be adversely affected. Firms of all sizes have erected international networks of corporate alliances, including joint ventures and partial ownership of independent firms, in order to gain access to new products and new technologies. Restrictions on foreign investment could well limit such cross-border deals in the United States, leaving the U.S. partners the losers.

U.S. national security interests would also be harmed. The countries that are the major sources of direct foreign investment in the United States—the United Kingdom, the Netherlands (and the Netherlands Antilles), Japan, Canada, West Germany— are all military allies as well. Suggestions that their citizens' purchases of American property or businesses are dangerous to "national security" can only cause consternation in countries that rely on the U.S. security umbrella. If they respond in kind, as their own domestic political pressures might well force them to, the commercial ties that have helped hold together the international security system of the market economies ever since World War II could be seriously weakened.

Even measures less restrictive than all-out bans on certain types of foreign direct investment would be ill advised. Take, for example, the "Bryant Amendment" to the 1988 trade bill, which was rejected by the House-Senate Conference Committee only after President Reagan made clear that it would precipitate a veto. This provision would have required foreign investors owning as little as 5 percent of a U.S. company or real property to provide the government with detailed information about their investment. Moreover, unlike almost all of the other firm-specific information the federal government collects, those individual company reports would have been subject to public disclosure. This would have given American-based firms, which need not disclose detailed information about their investments, a significant competitive advantage by providing them important intelligence about their foreign counterparts. The effect would surely have been to deter foreigners from investing in the United States.

The next president, then, faces a serious challenge in warding off misguided attempts to discourage foreign direct investment. A defensive response will not suffice. As has happened in the trade arena, the intensity of xenophobia is likely to make a defensive posture—piecemeal concessions limiting the activities of foreign investors in order to fend off more onerous and sweeping legislation—difficult to maintain. The best alternative is for the nation's leader to be frankly internationalist. The president must reaffirm, publicly and frequently, the importance of free flows of foreign investment in an economically interdependent world, and must use his media pulpit to begin the process of changing deepseated attitudes of economic isolationism.

This does not mean, however, that the United States should throw its economy wide open to all who would invest. There are two sets of considerations that might well justify government interference with foreigners' investment plans.

One is national security. While national security has become a much-abused rationale for all sorts of restrictions on international trade and investment flows, there is reason to keep certain firms whose work is critical to national defense from falling under the control of citizens of countries that do not maintain close defense ties with the United States. In practice, however, almost all acquisitions in which national security is a consideration emanate from countries that are U.S. allies. It is difficult for the U.S. government to assert that ownership by citizens of allied countries presents security risks, particularly at a time when the United States is demanding that its allies bear an increased responsibility for the common defense. The one recent attempt to make such a case arose in 1986, when then Commerce Secretary Malcolm Baldrige objected to the offer by Japan's Fujitsu to purchase U.S.–based Fairchild Electronics Corporation from Schlumberger, a French-controlled company based in the Netherlands Antilles, leaving the U.S. government in the impossible position of explaining why French ownership of a defense contractor is acceptable but Japanese ownership is not.

A general policy of prohibiting foreign ownership of defense firms is an open invitation to U.S. companies to acquire military contractors to protect themselves from unwanted foreign take-overs. A better approach, and one the U.S. government has followed in the past, is simply to require foreign purchasers of highly important defense firms to leave specific operations in the United States permanently, so the facilities will be available in case of war.[21] The government's Committee on Foreign Investment in the United States monitors such purchases, and should continue to do so.

The other consideration that justifies restrictions on foreign investment in the United States is reciprocity. Foreign direct investment, after all, allows foreigners to obtain a stream of future income from the United States. There is an inequity in granting citizens of some other country a claim on future income in the United States when that country refuses to offer Americans similar privileges, or in granting government con-tracts to foreign-owned firms with operations in the United States when American corporate subsidiaries are not entitled to obtain government contracts abroad. Where a country maintains policies that prevent U.S.–based firms from acquiring or estab-lishing domestic firms, the United States may have good reason to limit direct investment by that country's citizens in response. Foreign laws that allow corporations to restrict shareholding to citizens of their home countries also allow discrimination and should be opposed. Retaliation in other areas, such as trade, may be required to gain reciprocal rights to invest abroad.

The difficulty with pursuing a policy of restricting foreign investment from countries that restrict American investment is that there are no international understandings about which restrictions are legitimate and which are not. The United States has proposed that the General Agreement on Tariffs and Trade develop such a set of rules during its current negotiating round, which began in 1986. If the round does not produce significant progress on this complex issue, it might be necessary for the next president to press for a policy of reciprocity in foreign direct investment, either by the United States alone or in concert with a small number of other nations to which free flows of investment are important.

What the new president cannot do is turn the clock back. In the late 1980s, in a world with a large and growing degree of economic interdependence, questions of corporate nationality have come to possess little relevance. The physical location of a company's headquarters and the place of its incorporation are largely questions of historic accident and legal convenience, not matters of current economic importance. Most large firms, whether their headquarters are in Europe, North America, or Japan, operate with global scope, with employees of many nationalities, and produce earnings for shareholders all over the world. To distinguish among them according to the country in which each is based is to place an inappropriate emphasis on factors that simply no longer matter.

Notes

1. *New York Times*, November 27, 1987, p. D1; *Wall Street Journal*, July 27, 1987, p. 1; *Business Week*, August 3, 1987, p. 40, respectively.
2. Joyce Howe, "The Ugly 'Yellow Peril' Stigma Lives On," *New York Times*, April 11, 1988, p. A19.
3. *New York Times*, February 22, 1988, p. D1.
4. Martin Tolchin and Susan Tolchin, *Buying Into America* (New York: Times Books, 1988).
5. Edward John Ray, "The Determinants of Foreign Direct Investment in the United States: 1979–1985" (Paper presented to the National Bureau of Economic Research international trade conference, Cambridge, Mass., March 1988).

6. Robert E. Lipsey, *Changing Patterns of International Investment in and by the United States*, NBER Working Paper No. 2240 (Cambridge, Mass.: National Bureau of Economic Research, 1988).

7. U.S. affiliates of foreign companies imported $124.5 billion into the United States in 1986 and exported $50.7 billion. Ned G. Howenstine, "U.S. Affiliates of Foreign Companies: Operations in 1986," *Survey of Current Business*, vol. 68, no. 5 (May 1988), p. 68.

8. U.S.–based multinational companies imported $147 billion and exported $171 billion in 1986. Obie C. Whichard, "U.S. Multinational Corporations in 1986," *Survey of Current Business*, vol. 68, no. 6 (June 1988), p. 87.

9. Even investment banker Felix Rohatyn, well known as an internationalist, has warned, "[We] may have to look at some unpleasant choices unless there is a significant change in our financial condition and our relationship with the rest of the world." Felix Rohatyn, "Restoring American Independence," *New York Review of Books*, vol. 35, no. 2 (February 19, 1988), pp. 8–10.

10. Paul E. Sigmund, *Multinationals in Latin America: The Politics of Nationalization* (Madison: University of Wisconsin Press, 1980), p. 180.

11. Louis Uchitelle, "Overseas Spending by U.S. Companies Sets Record Pace," *New York Times*, May 20, 1988, p. A1.

12. Charles H. Kline and Co., Inc., *Chemical Strategies*, vol. 2, no. 8 (December 1986), p. 35.

13. Calculated based on data in *Survey of Current Business*, vol. 68, no. 6 (June 1988), p. 78.

14. Ellen M. Herr, "U.S. Business Enterprises Acquired or Established by Foreign Direct Investors in 1987," *Survey of Current Business*, vol. 68, no. 5 (May 1988), p. 50.

15. Calculated based on data in *Survey of Current Business*, vol. 67, no. 8 (August 1987), p. 98, and vol. 68, no. 6 (June 1988), p. 83.

16. For employment figures, see Howenstine, "U.S. Affiliates," *op. cit.*, p. 60.

17. *Survey of Current Business*, vol. 68, no. 6 (June 1988), p. 83.

18. Rachael McCulloch, "Japanese Investment in the United States," Brandeis University, 1988, mimeographed.

19. Ray, "Foreign Direct Investment," *op. cit.*

20. James J. O'Leary, "Trends in Foreign Investment in the United States and the Implications," United States Trust Company of New York, January 26, 1988, mimeographed.

21. Cynthia F. Mitchell, "Pentagon Eases Stand Against Foreign Stakes In U.S. Defense Firms," *Wall Street Journal*, April 28, 1988, p. 1.

10

The Four Years Ahead

Ever since the end of the Great Depression, Americans have taken a rising standard of living as their birthright. Each successive generation has enjoyed more disposable income, more leisure time, a greater stock of material possessions, and a wider array of government supports than its predecessors. In a way few Americans understand, the nation's ability to maintain that record is threatened by disturbing factors in the world economy. Making the hard economic choices required to keep the United States growing and to permit all groups within the population to share in that prosperity is the fundamental challenge of the post-Reagan era.

In some ways, the accomplishments of the eight-year administration of Ronald Reagan will support his successors in their efforts to achieve continued economic growth. President Reagan presided over an economic restructuring which caused extreme pain to many Americans, eliminating millions of jobs and forcing the shutdown of thousands of companies. In the process, however, it left the nation with a more mobile workforce and a more modern industrial plant. Reagan's attacks on government spending left Americans with reduced expectations of their government's capabilities, easing the political pressure on his successor to offer expensive new government-funded programs to cure social ills. And due to the cautious policies of the Federal

Reserve Board and the absence of unpleasant price shocks during his term, President Reagan is able to leave both an unusually low unemployment rate and a relatively low and stable rate of inflation to his successor, perhaps the most welcome gift of all.

In other ways, however, President Reagan leaves an exceptionally troubled economic legacy. Much of the prosperity of the past six years, since the bottom of the recession in November 1982, is due to the federal government's persistently spending more than it is taking in, by a very wide margin. Budget deficits are nothing new, of course, but the deficits of the Reagan era are different from those of earlier years, both qualitatively and quantitatively. In qualitative terms, the federal government has been spending a greater share of its income on military programs, income transfer payments such as social security, and interest payments on bonds issued to finance the deficits incurred in previous years. This has left a smaller share to fund the investments, from education to airport construction, that are essential to future economic growth. In quantitative terms, the Reagan budget deficits have amounted to a far greater proportion of the nation's total output than ever before in peacetime. They continue to command such a large share of the nation's savings that the United States remains a major importer of capital, a situation which led to an overvalued currency, a trade deficit so severe that it has greatly strengthened the forces of trade protectionism, and relatively high inflation-adjusted interest rates that have worsened the debt problems of developing countries.

This situation endangers not only living standards, but also America's customary role as the world's dominant power, shaping the course of events in distant corners of the globe. The ability to project diplomatic influence as well as military force depends upon the country's relative economic position in the world. "Economic strength," note two recent secretaries of state, "is . . . central to the way America is perceived by its friends and potential adversaries. U.S. political leadership in the world cannot be sustained if confidence in the American economy continues to be undermined by substantial trade and budget deficits."[1]

In sum, due largely to U.S. *domestic* economic policies, the world economy remains seriously out of balance. Restoring that balance will be the most crucial task of the next presidential administration.

What will it take? The first, and most critical, order of business is to pursue serious reductions in the federal budget deficit. This cannot be done through massive, recessionary spending cuts in a single year, but through a sustained program of budget reductions and tax increases over a four-year period. In order for there to be any chance of this being politically acceptable, the pain of deficit cutting will have to be spread equitably among the American people. Higher taxes will mean slower growth in household spending, but lower deficits should allow much lower interest rates, facilitating business expansion. This will gradually alter the division of the nation's income, reducing the share devoted to consumption and raising that invested in productive facilities. If deficit reduction is combined with less-restrictive monetary policy in the United States and diminished reliance on export-driven growth abroad, it could set the stage for another period of sustained prosperity in the 1990s.

The budget deficit will not resolve itself in the absence of major fiscal policy changes. Claims to the contrary assume that the federal government will dip into the growing surplus in the social security retirement and disability trust fund and apply it to current expenditures rather than reserving it to pay benefits in the second decade of the twenty-first century. Using social security funds in this way would be yet another example of fiscal indiscipline. Just as the children of the baby-boom generation will have to service the government debt accumulated in this decade to finance their parents' consumption, they would find themselves obligated to finance their parents' retirement because funds set aside for that purpose had been spent on other things instead.

While opposition to tax increases remains a potent political pledge, the evidence is clear that Americans are not willing to tolerate major cuts in the level of services they receive from the federal government. The public must be told the blunt truth: if they desire these programs and services, they must pay for them through higher taxes. In political terms, substantial increases in excise taxes on gasoline, tobacco, and alcoholic beverages, may be the most opportune way to begin, but they alone will not generate enough revenue to significantly narrow the budget deficit. Nor will raising taxes on the very rich. Undesirable as it is to reopen the federal income tax code once again, an increase of 1 percent or 2 percent in marginal personal income tax rates may be unavoidable. Alternatively, indexing of personal income taxes could be postponed.

On the spending side, significant cuts are possible only in the two largest budget categories, entitlements and defense. In the entitlements area, restricting medicare benefits to those with lower incomes is the easiest way to achieve major savings without eliminating the indexation that protects social security beneficiaries against inflation. On the defense side, the most important issue deals with fundamental military strategy. Almost all of America's strategic plans are based on the assumption that military spending will remain in the range of 6 percent of the nation's total output, as it has for most of the past thirty years. It may well prove impossible to maintain that level in the decade ahead, given the amount of taxes Americans are willing to pay. Yet reducing military spending under present circumstances is an endlessly frustrating task, because any reduction inevitably leaves the United States ill prepared to maintain a sound military posture under current strategic doctrines. There is a need to return to the beginning, developing new approaches to defense strategy based upon more modest budget assumptions— and then to seek bipartisan congressional consensus that spending should remain at that level for the foreseeable future.[2]

Second, the new administration must do all in its power to maintain an open world economy. Rising protectionism in the United States threatens to seriously erode America's standard of living, while the growth of barriers to trade abroad will make it difficult for the United States to attain the surplus it will need to service its foreign debts in the 1990s. Protectionism also hinders the adjustment of international trade flows to changes in exchange rates, contributing to the pressure to abandon a market-based exchange rate system.

Keeping the economy open will require careful maneuvering abroad and at home. With the Uruguay Round of multilateral trade negotiations off to a shaky start, the next president must do more to bring the private sector and Congress into the process. He must mobilize private sector support and keep Congress constantly apprised of the negotiations. The new administration must continue to push hard for visible signs of progress, even when it becomes more difficult as foreign countries' trade surpluses turn into deficits. Unless a new multilateral accord resolves basic issues of disagreement, trade frictions with Japan and the European Community are likely to escalate in the decade ahead, particularly as Europe moves toward unification in 1992 or soon thereafter. Yet the United States should not succumb to pressures to resolve trade frustrations through numerous bilateral accords. The break-up of the world trading system into regional blocs, each based upon separate bilateral agreements, is directly contrary to the long-established U.S. goal of liberalizing the international flow of goods and services. By making it more difficult to import and export, this strategy could have an adverse effect on living standards in the United States.

A major lesson of the past decade is that it is not enough for a president to negotiate freer trade with other countries. He must also attend to the domestic front on trade matters. The next president must convince Congress and the public that he is according trade matters their due priority and is protecting American interests by dealing severely with trading partners who infringe upon the rules. The political structure for handling trade issues requires that the president take the lead in order to protect members of Congress from intense pressure to save local factories and mines from import competition.[3] When the chief executive fails to assume the role of advocate and lightning rod on trade matters, as was the case throughout the Reagan years, the protectionist pressures are almost impossible for Congress to withstand.

Domestic policies to ease the pain of adjusting to economic change are an important but often neglected component of the drive to liberalize international trade. The new administration cannot be guilty of the same neglect. Toward this end, new efforts to retrain displaced workers and to encourage them to move to areas where their skills are in demand must be part and parcel of the adjustment process. Existing government programs have, by and large, failed to teach displaced workers useful skills and to move them into jobs that do not entail substantial loss of income. New ideas and new experiments are badly needed. Once a new program is in place, the next president should seek to phase out programs that shelter U.S. industries from international competition or encourage uneconomic production. These programs redistribute income within the United States at a substantial loss to economic efficiency—the cost of protecting agriculture is equal to 3 percent of total farm output, and protection for the steel industry cost the U.S. economy $2 billion in 1985[4]—while causing both producers and workers to make economically unwise decisions.

Keeping the economy open also means encouraging the flow of private investment across international borders. The new administration must vigorously attack the resurgent chauvinism that finds foreign investment in American farms and factories somehow to be harmful to the United States. But, at the same time, it must insist that if foreign citizens have the opportunity to invest in the United States without discrimination, Americans should have precisely the same opportunities abroad.

The third major economic challenge confronting the new administration is the need to rebuild international economic institutions so that they may be relevant in the world of the twenty-first century. This painful process will offer few short-term rewards, but it is essential if the trend towards greater economic integration among the world's market economies is to be maintained.

The international organizations created in the wake of World War II have long since ceased to function as they did when the United States was the the world's dominant economic power. The General Agreement on Tariffs and Trade, which covers a decreasing share of world trade, can be revitalized only if its members are successful in achieving major breakthroughs during the Uruguay Round. The Bretton Woods Agreement, establishing fixed exchange rates, has long since been abandoned, to be replaced first by limited floating, then by freely floating currencies and then, since 1985, by ad hoc agreements among major countries to control the level of the dollar—agreements which, unfortunately, have kept the U.S. currency from falling farther despite the continued large U.S. trade deficit. As Europe moves to establish a central bank and Japan becomes accustomed to its new role as the world's largest international creditor, the door may be opened to new ideas about the functioning of the international exchange rate system.

The other two Bretton Woods institutions, the World Bank and the International Monetary Fund, are in disarray, occasioned in good part by their continuing ineffectiveness in resolving the massive debt problems of the developing world. Their inability to address the debt problem save by prescribing orthodox free market economic reforms points to the need for a fundamental rethinking of their role in the world economy. At the same time, the United States should recommit itself to support these institutions. The issue is political as well as economic. If the United States reduces its participation in the World Bank or seeks to diminish the institution's importance, it creates an opportunity for other nations to expand their economic influence as America's contracts.

A less well known international institution, the Bank for International Settlements, has made a major contribution to improved economic stability by beginning the arduous task of bringing the banking regulations of the world's major financial nations into harmony. The new administration should wholeheartedly support this effort. It should also encourage similar actions among securities regulators. The world is in many ways becoming a single financial market. Regulatory inconsistencies among nations, however, can put some investors at a disadvantage in doing business abroad, and they give rise to undesirable side effects, most significantly the possibility that loose regulation in one country will contribute to the collapse of financial institutions in countries halfway around the globe. Again, the Congress, which has been struggling unsuccessfully to write a comprehensive banking bill for the past six years, will have to be convinced to play a constructive role in this process.

Stepping up to these challenges will be difficult under conditions of economic prosperity. It will be even more difficult if the six-year-old economic expansion in the United States comes to an end early in the next presidential term. Recession will sharply increase the budget deficit by reducing income tax revenues and augmenting demands on social programs, and it will give renewed strength to forces of protection and economic isolation who will surely seek to blame foreigners for the loss of U.S. jobs. Yet the threat of recession is all the more reason to proceed quickly with the unpleasant task of reducing the imbalances in the U.S. economy. Under present circumstances, the government's economic tools are not available to deal with a declining economy: monetary policy has been committed to stabilize the dollar's exchange rate at unrealistic levels, while expansionary fiscal policy measures would require a further increase in a budget deficit that is already unacceptably large. Reducing the budget deficit and with it the trade deficit would ease the pressures on both monetary and fiscal policy in subsequent years, increasing the government's ability to use either or both to counteract recession.

In implementing these policies, the next president needs to work more closely with other major countries from the outset of his administration on economic as well as defense matters. Former President Nixon's proposal that the first undertaking of the newly elected president should be to spend two weeks with America's European allies should not be taken in jest.[5] Basic forums for intergovernmental cooperation, from the annual economic summit meetings of national leaders to the semiannual meetings of trade ministers, are already in place. While the United States no longer has the power to compel its major trading partners to act as it desires, it still is recognized as a leader and its ideas command attention. After all, the United States is the world's only superpower in both economic and military affairs. But following years of failure to live up to its promises that the budget deficit would be addressed, the United lacks credibility with its trading partners. The new administration will bear the burden of convincing other nations of the sincerity and worth of its initiatives and commitments.

International cooperation will be complicated by America's new relationship with other industrial countries. The European Community now has a combined national income comparable to that of the United States, and Japan is closing the gap. Although both have an abiding interest in promoting a stable global economy, neither has taken the lead to ensure it. Each will have to bear more responsibility for the smooth functioning of the world economy. Joint leadership will be necessary. Joint leadership is less stable and more prone to delay than leadership exercised by a single dominant country. Nevertheless, all countries have common concerns and common interests. Each has a vital stake in the management of interdependence, because its welfare depends on other countries as never before.

An important step both in devising the new administration's economic programs and in convincing the world of their seriousness is the selection of economic policy staff who are competent, respected, and nondogmatic. On such issues as trade and management of developing country debt, poor staff work has plagued the Reagan administration, leading to impractical or ill-conceived negotiating proposals and an inability to offer constructive responses to proposals by other countries. The general quality of appointees, particularly in fields related to foreign affairs, has declined during the Reagan years due to the increased use of political criteria in their selection. As a former Republican diplomat and cabinet member has suggested, "A contributing factor has been the elimination from the pool of eligible prospects those who cannot meet the ideological litmus test."[6] In addition, a greater proportion of Reagan administration appointees have resigned after a relatively brief period in office; the average tenure of Senate-confirmed appointees, almost three years during the administration of President Lyndon Johnson and two-and-a-half years under President Carter, has been only two years during Reagan's time in office.[7] In international economic affairs, this has resulted in U.S. officials with little institutional knowledge or historical understanding negotiating with far better informed foreign emissaries, much to the disadvantage of the United States.

The staffing problem extends beyond political appointments, to the civil service. After twelve years of government by presidents who ran against the Washington establishment and demeaned the abilities of those who chose to work for the federal government, many of the best and brightest no longer seek out federal service. Improving the caliber of career government workers is less a matter of money than of attitude. It is important to restore the sense that employment in the government sector can make important contributions to the nation's well-being. Only the president can do so.

As international economic affairs come to have ever greater influence over the state of the domestic economy, the question of who will represent America's interest in international economic negotiations looms ever more important. The United States needs to develop a cadre of career specialists in international economic policy, who could provide continuity and negotiating expertise in senior civil service and subcabinet positions. Greater stability among support staff and negotiators is vital if the United States is to hold its own in consultations with countries such as Japan and Britain, whose representatives often bring decades of preparation to the bargaining table. Candidates for key appointive posts in international economic affairs should be recruited without regard to party affiliation, with a high premium placed not only on knowledge, but also on substantive experience dealing with economic issues on an international plane. As a recent book on the making of foreign economic policy notes pointedly: ". . . the United States must soberly face the question whether in the closing years of the twentieth century a system of international economic relations can be fashioned and run by amateurs, even by brilliant and well-intentioned amateurs, recruited for a brief stint in positions of power."[8]

Along with better staffing, the new administration must reexamine the organizational arrangements within which economic policy decisions are made. Although the Reagan administration has made extensive use of interagency economic task forces at the cabinet, subcabinet, and staff levels, there has been little opportunity to examine the interrelated effects of trade, monetary, and investment policies. No attempt was made to coordinate economic issues in a fashion similar to the National Security Council's coordination of defense and diplomatic matters. Only late in the Reagan years did the increasing influence of Treasury Secretary James A. Baker III result in many of the strands of economic policy being gathered together in one place.

The blurring of the distinction between foreign investment and foreign trade, the growing diplomatic ramifications of trade policy, the interdependence of trade and financial flows, and the increasingly frequent conflict between security concerns and international economic concerns make it desirable to establish an international economic policy council in the White House. The council, with a staff reporting to the president, would be charged with coordinating decisionmaking on international economic concerns and bringing harmony to the policies of the diverse agencies involved, from the Department of Defense to the Department of Agriculture to the Office of the the U.S. Trade Representative.

Realistically, titles and positions on organization charts will not determine how decisions are made. In any administration, power will flow to those officials who best understand how to wield it. But, as the experience of past administrations, notably that of Richard Nixon, has shown, an energetic and politically astute staff that coordinates deliberations on international economic issues can have a salutary effect. The Nixon administration's Council on International Economic Policy, established in 1971, had a small staff, but through high-level meetings each morning and special working groups to tackle major issues, it managed to coordinate the activities of the Treasury and the U.S. Trade Representative. As two participants relate, "Once a single overall structure was in place to resolve broad issues in policy, assignments of day-to-day responsibilities for particular issues created fewer jealousies and bureaucratic rivalries."[9] Although it will by no means resolve all problems and conflicts, such a structure deserves emulation.

At the same time, the new administration should resist proposals to establish a cabinet-level department of trade combining the negotiating duties of the U.S. Trade Representative with the Commerce Department's responsibilities to promote exports and rule on complaints that foreigners are engaging in unfair practices in sales to the United States. The Commerce Department, which would likely become the heart of the new agency, has in recent years been extremely sympathetic to claims by U.S. companies that unfair foreign practices are the source of their competitive problems, and has little record of taking broader national interests into account in its advocacy. Putting all responsibilities for trade matters in a new department could make the thrust of U.S. trade policy far more protectionist and mute the voices of those presently charged with finding ways to reduce the restrictions impeding foreign trade.

Reorienting the nation's international economic policy will not be possible without much closer cooperation between the executive branch and Congress. It is here, most of all, that the efforts of recent U.S. administrations have fallen short.

Instinctively, members of the executive branch tend to regard Congress as an obstacle to the making of economic policy, not as a partner. Among conservatives, a narrow constitutionalism holds that the international realm in particular is the exclusive province of the president, and that attempts to exert congressional influence should be kept at bay. But the truth is that in foreign economic policy, just as in other aspects of foreign affairs, only policies enjoying broad, bipartisan support are likely to meet with success. Constitutional jurisprudence aside, the hard fact is that if Congress is not adequately consulted as decisions of international economic import are made, it has the ability to blunt many key presidential initiatives. That happened repeatedly during the latter years of the Reagan administration. Congressional dissatisfaction with the president's management of trade issues resulted in passage of a trade bill to which the president had a strong objection, while congressional frustration with the administration's reluctance to be more active in resolving developing country debt problems was demonstrated by delaying approval of an increase in the U.S. contribution to the capital of the World Bank.

Working more closely with Congress will most assuredly not be easy. Internal reforms have diffused power widely within both the Senate and the House of Representatives. Dozens of committees and subcommittees have jurisdiction over some aspect of international economic relations, and the weakening of the seniority system means that the executive branch cannot assume that a handful of leaders can make commitments for their members. A reduction in the number of congressional subcommittees might make relations less contentious, but such a reform does not appear to be in the cards.

Yet the task of maintaining close cooperation with Congress on international economic matters is not impossible. By and large, members of Congress expect and wish the initiative on foreign economic policy to come from the president; their desire, aside from closer consultation, is that the president shield them from constituent pressures to favor immediate local concerns over broader national interests.

This suggests two essential components to better relations with the congressional branch. The administration should consult regularly with congressional leaders of both parties on issues of trade, exchange rate policy and relations with multilateral lending institutions in an attempt to establish a bipartisan consensus, much as it does on military and foreign policy concerns. Encouraging closer congressional involvement with GATT negotiations, including appointing individual members of Congress as part of the U.S. negotiating team, would be a good way to start. And the administration should understand that if individual senators and representatives are to support society's interest in an open world economy over the more parochial interests of individual companies or groups of workers, they must be able to demonstrate their responsiveness to constituent concerns in the process. The president must repeatedly inform the public not just of the economic benefits of an open economy, but also of the steps the government is taking to address unfairness abroad and to aid those harmed by trade liberalization at home. Congressionally mandated programs to aid displaced workers and studies of how imports are harming specific industries are a small price to pay for maintaining political support for a liberal economic order.

Dealing with the three overriding economic challenges ahead—reducing the federal government's budget deficit, maintaining an open world economy, and rebuilding international economic institutions—will do little to boost the political popularity of the new administration. There are few votes to be gained from increasing taxes, negotiating trade liberalization agreements, and redefining the role of the World Bank. Righting the imbalance in the world economy necessarily means slowing the growth rate of personal consumption in the United States, which translates directly into fewer new cars, shorter vacation trips, and less frequent meals out. The negative reaction from voters is unlikely to be mitigated by promises that the shift from a consumption-driven to an investment-driven economy will allow for greater growth in consumption in years ahead.

Yet the alternatives are not pleasant to contemplate. Sooner or later, foreigners will cease to be willing to lend their money to finance consumption in the United States. Under present conditions, that would force interest rates much higher, choking off business investment and rapidly driving the United States into recession. Higher interest rates and fewer export opportunities would force developing country debtors into default, endangering the stability of major banks. That, and the failure of many companies that have acquired excessive loads of debt, could drag the economies of other nations down as well. An upsurge in protectionism and a disintegration of global economic ties would surely follow, which, in turn, would not bode well for the next president's prospects for reelection in 1992.

One way or another, the world economy will find its way to a state of better international balance. With forceful, farsighted leadership, and credible changes in policy, the new American president can help those changes occur in an environment of economic growth rather than economic decline.

Notes

1. Henry Kissinger and Cyrus Vance, "Bipartisan Objectives for American Foreign Policy," *Foreign Affairs*, vol 66, no. 5 (Summer 1988), p. 910.
2. For a brief discussion of this issue, see Michael Blumenthal, et al., *Fiscal Policy and Foreign Policy* (Washington, D.C.: Johns Hopkins School of Advanced International Studies, 1988).
3. I. M. Destler, *American Trade Politics: System Under Stress* (Washington, D.C.: Institute for International Economics/New York: Twentieth Century Fund, 1986).
4. World Bank, *World Development Report 1988* (New York, Oxford University Press, 1988), p. 16.
5. Richard M. Nixon, *1999: Victory Without War* (New York: Simon and Schuster, 1988), p. 207.
6. Elliot Richardson, "Civil Servants: Why Not the Best?" *Wall Street Journal*, November 20, 1987, page 26.
7. Ibid., quoting Survey by the National Academy of Public Administration.

8. Raymond Vernon and Deborah L. Spar, *Beyond Globalism: Remaking American Foreign Economic Policy* (New York: Free Press, 1988).

9. George P. Shultz and Kenneth W. Dam, *Economic Policy: Beyond the Headlines* (New York: Norton Press, 1978), p. 177.

Priorities and Prescriptions for the Next President: Members of the Study Group Speak Out

Priorities and Prescriptions for the Next President

Robert D. Hormats

On Matching Resources and Responsibilities

From time to time in history, shifts in the configuration of international economic strength are so great that changes in the roles of nations are required to ensure that resources and responsibilities are closely matched. That was true after World War I, when the United States inherited economic and political power from Great Britain. It is true today.

The increasingly broad distribution of economic strength in the world, and improvements in East-West relations, challenge traditional ways of thinking about the exercise of American leadership. There is a clear need to strike a better balance between the benefits nations receive from a prosperous world economy and from collective Western security and their contributions to them. But this cannot be achieved—as it might have been in earlier decades—as the result of U.S. requests or demands. U.S. leadership now must be exercised by building international coalitions in support of American objectives. Others must see a better balance as being in their common interest. And the probability of their doing so will be enhanced considerably if the president puts forward a strategy that both underscores the enormous progress the West has made by adhering to shared economic, political, and defense principles, and demonstrates a willingness to ensure our partners a share in managing alliances and global economic institutions which is equivalent to the costs and burdens we are asking them to bear.

While still possessing by far the greatest combination of industrial, political, and military power in the world, the United States is no longer the preeminent economic force it was in past decades. The leader of the West is now its largest debtor, whereas for most of the postwar period it was its major creditor and benefactor. In contrast, other nations have attained formidable financial and trading strength, and their economic successes now permit them considerable independence of action. Alliances which have been the basis for Western security and prosperity for the last forty years operate in a very different environment today. Many Europeans see the Soviets as a diminishing military threat and a more attractive trading partner, reducing their enthusiasm for additional defense spending. Western Europe and Japan are asserting themselves to a greater degree on the world political and economic stage. Concerns are growing about the world fragmenting into commercial blocs.

In the past, alliances that were instrumental in containing the Soviets militarily also served to contain economic friction between the United States and other industrialized democracies. Western leaders could point to the necessity of alliance cohesion in the face of the Soviet menace as an argument for compromising even the most acrimonious economic disputes—often, some Americans would assert, in a way that did not serve U.S. trade interests. The common fear of the Soviets was also instrumental in enabling NATO leaders to obtain public support in their countries for increased military expenditures.

In the future, however, the West may find that it cannot rally its peoples around a pastel banner. Without a shared sense of a serious Soviet threat to justify contributions to the collective defense or to motivate efforts to settle intra-alliance economic differences, there is a substantial risk of centrifugal forces taking hold. Frictions over burden-sharing are likely to become more acrimonious as Americans debate whether this country has the resources, or the will, to play a leadership role of the size and the scope of earlier years. Enter the new INF agreement, plus

Gorbachev's talk of a "common European house," and we are seeing renewed concerns in Europe about a "decoupling" of the United States from the defense of the continent. On the economic front, Europe and Japan fear the new U.S. trade bill will be implemented in a protectionist fashion; Americans, Canadians, and Asians are concerned about limits on their future access to the unified European market planned for 1992; and Japan is seen abroad as establishing closer ties with the developing nations of East Asia, perhaps in the process of squeezing others out.

While the global economic and political environment is changing, U.S. leadership still remains a vital prerequisite for progress. Washington must convey a vision for NATO, and for its other security relationships, that does not depend wholly on fear of the Soviet Union; it must address a broad range of economic, political, and social interests in order to retain a strong consensus in support of defense cooperation. Specifically, the United States should seek a reaffirmation by its allies that the prosperity of the West is indivisible and, based thereon, engage them more enthusiastically in the effort to sustain world economic growth, to promote a better balance in the global economy, and to reduce distortions in the international flow of goods, services, and investment. And it should forge a common Western approach to take advantage of potential opportunities to negotiate new arms reduction agreements, and improve political and economic ties, with Moscow while maintaining allied political harmony, strong collective security, and a firm commitment to close cooperation among market economies.

At a time in history when the West has a unique opportunity to improve relations with the Soviets, and the Chinese, its own cohesion on both economic and security issues is particularly important. It is precisely because the Western economic system has demonstrated its superiority to the state-dominated one of the communist world—and threatens to relegate it to prolonged technological inferiority—that pressure for economic reform is so strong in the East. And preservation of a strong Western alliance, despite periods of economic stress, has been a major inducement to the Kremlin to participate in arms reduction negotiations. A deterioration in economic cooperation among the industrialized democracies, for example a resort to protectionism or an outbreak of financial instability, would weaken Western prosperity, decrease pressures on the Soviets for change, and reduce the attractiveness of the West's economic model. It would invite Moscow to try to play one ally off against another, and jeopardize our cohesion.

One threat to our common interests today is that policies will be based on a set of assumptions, or myths, that lead to defensive or inward-looking approaches to the world, foster greater nationalism, and divert attention from the effort to achieve a broader sharing of responsibility both for Western security and for a well-functioning world economy. In order to forge an international strategy that will further America's global interests, the next president will need first to clearly dispel three of these myths.

Myth one: America is in decline. In the early 1980s, the U.S. economy went through a tough time—and it still suffers from big budget and trade deficits. For the most part, however, these are the result of distortive policies rather than of an underlying deterioration. On the positive side, the U.S. economy has demonstrated a remarkable resilience, a formidable ability to create new jobs through sustained noninflationary growth, and a capacity to reward innovative entrepreneurs. These are not the signs of a deteriorating economy.

The recovery of Western Europe and Japan after World War II and the dynamic growth of several East Asian nations have, of course, reduced America's share of world gross national product (GNP). Yet that shrinkage was bound to occur as economic activity picked up in the rest of the world. Restoring prosperity among friendly nations abroad was a primary goal of American postwar policy and one of its great successes. Had other nations not progressed, America's portion of the global product would have been greater, but our absolute level of prosperity would have been far less. Moreover, had our allies not recovered, had the feared domino effect occurred in Asia after Vietnam, and were those nations now suffering from economic weakness and instability, America's global defense burden would be much greater than it is today.

Myth two: America's recent economic problems are the fault of other countries. Americans are justifiably concerned about how slow other nations have been to lower trade barriers, to assume a greater share of the global security burden, and to provide more assistance to developing countries. But placing excessive blame on them diverts attention from putting our own house in order. If the United States does not close the gap between savings and investment and between consumption and production, which requires us *inter alia* to substantially cut our budget deficit, and if we fail to boost our productivity and educational standards, no action by any group of nations will help us much.

Myth three: the West cannot keep up with Soviet military expenditures, and America is overextended in the world, so to save money we must quickly reach another arms agreement with Moscow and reduce our military presence abroad. In fact, the West as a whole is better able to finance current, or, if need be, increased defense expenditures, and generate new military technologies, than is the Soviet Union. The issue is not one of capabilities but of the necessity or desirability of additional military spending in view of the overall strategic environment. And whether the United States is militarily overextended abroad is not a question that can be answered only by examining numbers; it also requires a close look at the nature and the degree of the threats to U.S. interests. We can surely utilize our military budget more efficiently at home and abroad than we have in recent years; we also can and should better share costs and responsibilities with allies whose interests we defend, for example by keeping sea lanes open. That is an argument for using power and money more resourcefully and negotiating new arrangements with allies, not for pulling back precipitously from overseas commitments or hastily making another arms reduction agreement with Moscow simply to save money. There may indeed be opportunities for reducing America's military presence abroad and for negotiating cuts in our armaments, but these should be decided on the basis of security considerations.

Recognizing that actions based on such myths will not serve U.S. interests, how then should the president proceed? The responsibility sharing needed both to make the world economy work better and to put U.S. security alliances on a sounder basis will not happen spontaneously. It requires that the president take crisp and clear initiatives to forge the necessary international consensus, and to harness the new strengths of its trading partners, in three important areas.

Trade: The twelve members of the European Community are now engaged in establishing a single internal market. Ideally, the United States and others should view this as a positive development, because it will make Europe more dynamic, a stronger ally, and an expanding market for imported goods. But because European officials have suggested that they will seek "reciprocity" from trading partners in key sectors and the Community is moving to negotiate both membership agreements with other Western European countries and preferential trade arrangements with Comecon nations, outsiders are increasingly concerned about future access to the European market. The growing use of market-sharing, or "voluntary restraint," agreements by virtually all nations adds to global trade distortions. And there will be difficulties in reducing the $171 billion U.S. trade deficit; if Americans become frustrated by the slowness of progress, there may be calls here for protection or subsidies against other nations; industries abroad may seek similar measures as their sales to the United States shrink and more American or Third World exports enter their home markets.

In this environment, achieving U.S. objectives in the current Uruguay Round of trade negotiations—such as lowering barriers and subsidies in agriculture, reducing impediments to trade in services, establishing stricter rules to protect intellectual property, and improving procedures for resolving disputes—will require an especially active and high-level U.S. effort, which on occasion will involve the president. It will also mean establishing common ground with important developing economies, such as Brazil, China, Mexico, Singapore, and South Korea, which must be included in the process of making global trading rules just as they must be expected to abide by those rules. It may be necessary for a few nations that wish to reduce trade barriers in certain areas to do so vis-à-vis one another, even if a majority of nations do not go along and, therefore, do not share in the benefits. Although this violates traditional most-favored-nation principles, it may be the only way to make progress in key sectors. In the Nuclear Non-Proliferation Treaty of 1970, a similar approach was taken to prevent one or two nations from holding up agreement; while many nuclear powers subscribed, others did not, although they were permitted to sign on later.

To give impetus to American trade initiatives, and raise trade to a level of "high policy"—which is necessary due to its economic and foreign policy importance—the president should, early in his administration, convene and personally chair a summit of leaders of major industrialized and developing nations to give top-level impetus to trade negotiations. President Kennedy's support was critical in the round that bears his name; the new president should make these negotiations a major priority.

Redefining global security responsibilities: NATO needs to strengthen conventional forces following the elimination of intermediate-range nuclear missiles. The Europeans, however, do not necessarily share the view that increased expenditures to equip such forces are warranted, especially as East-West relations improve. Nor have they demonstrated a willingness to integrate military production and procurement, and establish integrated weapons systems, which would better utilize their defense budgets. Europeans also point out that while the United States accounts for 70 percent of the West's military expenditures, Europe collectively provides about 60 percent of Western military manpower and about the same percentage of total ground forces. There is danger of future friction between the United States and Western Europe not only over burden-sharing but also over the pace of economic normalization with Moscow, the nature of the Soviet threat, and whether Europe's voice in NATO should be strengthened if it accepts a great financial role.

The issue with Japan is quite different. That nation's defense expenditures, much lower as a percentage of GNP than that of Europe, and its naval role are growing—but as numbers and capabilities increase, Japan's neighbors have become concerned and constitutional hurdles are raised at home.

Here, as in trade relations, U.S. leadership remains critical. Washington should initiate a ministerial-level examination, in

NATO, of the goals and the nature of Western security cooperation in a changing economic and political environment. NATO must determine whether its capabilities in Europe and other parts of the world are matched both to its missions and to the potential threat, and whether the costs of financing those capabilities is appropriately shared. If the United States reduces its budget deficit, as Europeans correctly urge it to do, and as it must do in its own interest, restraints will inevitably be placed on its defense spending. Then the issue of burden-sharing will become particularly acute. Europe must come to terms with the military responsibilities resulting from its economic success, even as the United States comes to terms with its own resource constraints. NATO must also concert on a strategy for further arms reductions talks with Moscow, and bring Japan—whose defense role in the Pacific is growing—more into the picture on such matters.

NATO, plus Japan, should hammer out a consensus on economic relations with the Soviet Union. Moscow has indicated an interest in observer status in the General Agreement on Tariffs and Trade (GATT) and the International Monetary Fund (IMF). While this may for the moment be premature, the West should take the initiative to try to bring the Soviets into a framework of less formal, consultative arrangements that would, over time, increase Moscow's incentive to play by global trade, investment, and financial rules; that would increase the predictability of Soviet actions and reduce the possibility that they will play one Western economy against another. It will also permit business relations to proceed between East and West on a sound and mutually beneficial basis.

Allied cooperation must also include increased assistance to developing nations—whose growth and social stability is extremely important to the West. A significant increase in Japanese and Western European economic support both for the heavily indebted countries, whose democratic systems or political stability is threatened by their financial predicament, and for the world's poorest countries would be a contribution to vital Western objectives. U.S., European, and Japanese aid collaboration would also add a moral dimension to their relationship that would be especially appealing to younger people who downplay the significance of security ties. It should be very much a part of the broader effort to share responsibility, which is required by the relative shift in economic strength.

Sharing costs will involve sharing power in important areas where the United States is unaccustomed to doing so. If Europe and Japan contribute a greater share of overseas economic assistance, they will want greater influence in global economic institutions, such as the World Bank. Likewise, if they take on a greater share of Western defense costs, they understandably will want more of a voice in the decisionmaking process in that area; they will also insist on enjoying a greater share of the market for weapons and other defense items.

Promoting policy compatibility and monetary reform: The next president will inherit an economy that is burdened by massive foreign and domestic debts, that is heavily dependent on inflows of foreign capital, and that is likely to experience large trade deficits for years to come. The seven-nation economic summits, and close cooperation among the finance ministers and central bank governors of those countries, have succeeded in reducing global trade imbalances, and have helped to guide currencies toward more sustainable relationships. The next step is to build a firmer structure for achieving compatibility among national economic policies. Such policies are formulated by governments, which must be responsive to voters whose economic prescriptions often differ considerably from country to country. Frequently, policy cooperation has faltered because the United States assumed that it knew better how to run the economies of other countries than they did themselves, and other nations felt they knew best what was good policy for the United States.

A better collective understanding of how each major economy responds to different domestic policy measures is required, along with a consensus on adherence to economic "performance indicators" among the Group of Seven nations. For the foreseeable future, domestic demand abroad must exceed that in the United States, while consumption in this country must slow relative to savings and investment, if the U.S. trade deficit and large foreign surpluses are to be steadily reduced without inflation here or recession abroad. In this environment, the exchange rate regime should evolve from the current one (in which finance ministers periodically agree on a temporary set of exchange rates, or a "holding zone") toward one based on a longer-term "reference" or "target zone"—linked to a basket of goods or commodities and backed up by currency "war chests," which would be mobilized when underlying economic conditions do not justify changes in exchange rates or when intervention is needed to reduce short-term volatility. This would give the market greater confidence in exchange rate stability. It would enable potential investors in new plants and equipment, as well as importers and exporters, to make judgments based on the expectation of relative currency stability—whereas now such decisions are frequently postponed because volatility has degraded the credibility of any given exchange rate and thus has slowed the shifts in trade and investment that currency changes were intended to promote. Because the European Community is examining the notion of a European Central Bank, it will, at a minimum, be important to ensure that this integrates smoothly into the global monetary system.

The new president should make currency stability a medium-term priority. It would reassure potential investors in new productive capacity in the United States—which is needed to meet rising export demand—that their investments will not turn unprofitable from a sharply higher dollar, as happened in the early 1980s. But he will also want to avoid prematurely attempting to stabilize the dollar—a move that in early 1987 exacerbated market uncertainty and forced up U.S. interest rates.

Finally, to foster a steady reduction in the U.S. trade deficit and maintain a smooth inflow of capital, the United States will need to conduct a special dialogue with its largest creditor, Japan. This should include annual meetings between the president and the prime minister, and ongoing U.S.–Japan cabinet and congressional sessions. The enormous financial and commercial interdependence between these two nations gives them a common interest in avoiding constant acrimony on individual economic issues, in averting mutually disruptive actions, and in working together to address the economic problems of the Third World.

With economic power increasingly diffused, allied compliance with American wishes can be neither assumed nor demanded. It must result from the president's willingness to dismiss those myths which turn America inward and instead take initiatives to foster shared responsibility for the world economy and increased support for a strong Western defense, even as the West pursues opportunities for improving relations with the Soviet Union. Depending on his success, the United States will enter the twenty-first century either as the confident leader of a strong Western alliance and a prosperous world economy, or as a great power in retreat.

Robert D. Hormats is currently vice chairman of Goldman Sachs International Corporation. Previously, he was assistant secretary of state for economic and business affairs. He has also served as deputy U.S. trade representative with the rank of ambassador and as senior staff member for economic policy with the National Security Council.

Leonard Silk

On the Twin Deficits and National Security

The connection between a nation's internal and external deficits is clear: if a nation invests more than it saves and consumes more than it produces—as the United States has been doing—the excess must be covered by an inflow of foreign savings. The greater the internal budget deficit, the lower the rate of national savings and the greater the dependence on foreign capital.

America's huge budget and trade deficits have hampered its leadership of the noncommunist world, and could jeopardize the security of the international economic and military alliance that has given us peace and prosperity for the past four decades. The highest priority of the next president is to strengthen the national economy while working with our allies to sustain the international economic and defense system.

To remedy the nation's external economic weakness, the U.S. structural budget deficit must be reduced, and if possible eliminated; structural balance means that, in the vicinity of full employment, the budget should be at least in balance or preferably in surplus, given America's need to service and amortize its greatly swollen foreign debt.

Restoration of structural balance cannot be achieved in a single year; to attempt to do so would almost certainly impose extreme deflationary and recessionary pressures on the American economy and the rest of the world. Nevertheless, steady progress toward budgetary balance over the next four years is a highly important objective in restoring the nation's external equilibrium and reducing its dependence on the inflow of foreign capital.

There does appear to be a political consensus that the budget deficit must be eliminated. There is, however, no consensus on how to do it. The conflict between Republicans and Democrats on that issue was widened during the 1988 presidential campaign by Vice President George Bush's pledge not to raise taxes, while Governor Michael Dukakis left open the option of raising taxes if expenditures could not be cut enough to close the budgetary gap in the next four years. But, whoever is in the White House, the primary stress will be on reducing expenditures rather than raising taxes. This may or may not be wise, but I take it as a political reality. And that reality will also mean even tighter constraints on defense than on nondefense outlays.

While the unified budget deficit, as estimated by the Congressional Budget Office, is projected to decline, under current policies, from $136 billion (2.9 percent of GNP) in fiscal year 1990 to $121 billion (2.0 percent of GNP) by 1993, Richard N. Brandon, staff director of the U.S. Senate Budget Committee, notes that the real outlook is less promising for the following reasons. First, the projection assumes no recession during the next four years. Second, it assumes no real growth in military spending—a significant cut below Secretary of Defense Frank Carlucci's projection of a 2 percent annual real growth after fiscal year 1989, which already implies a four-year reduction of about $250 billion in the buildup planned by Defense Secretary Caspar Weinberger during the earlier Reagan years. Third, and most important, the projected decline in the unified budget results mainly from a rise in the social security surplus from about 1 percent of GNP in fiscal year 1989 to 1.5 percent of GNP in 1993. In an analysis prepared for the Council on Foreign Relations, Mr. Brandon concludes that, without policy changes, the non-social-security deficit will remain above $220 billion through fiscal year 1993; and, eliminating the optimistic assumptions cited above, the real structural deficit would remain at about 4 percent of GNP.

How can this unacceptable gap be closed? Can cuts be made in nondefense programs? It appears probable that, given the pile-up of acute problems, outlays are more likely to rise for education; research; health; welfare reform; reducing toxic wastes and other pollutants; improving airports, bridges, and other infrastructures—outlays which are unlikely to be fully offset by cuts in other social programs. Both presidential candidates in the 1988 campaign, reflecting widespread public and business sentiment, voiced support for expanding outlays for areas that have been underfunded in recent years, with damage to the nation's human capital, its productivity growth, and its competitiveness in world markets.

Can the social security surplus be widened to narrow the unified budget deficit? That appears highly improbable. Even if Congress resists political pressures to reduce the social security surplus by improving benefits or reducing payroll taxes, it would be difficult to imagine its cutting benefits or raising taxes to increase the already growing social security surplus significantly, in order to reduce the unified budget deficit.

Can federal interest payments be cut? They seem more likely to rise. President Reagan's own budget for fiscal year 1989 estimated that net budgetary costs of federal interest payments will rise from $135 billion in fiscal year 1989 to $141 billion in 1991. With current account deficits and federal budget deficits slated to continue adding to the total debt, even on optimistic assumptions, it appears likely that net interest payments included in the federal budget will exceed $150 billion by 1993. The prospects of a fall in interest rates that would overcome the effects of continued heavy federal borrowing at home and abroad appear slight.

Hence, the effort to cut federal expenditures seems bound to focus on defense expenditures. The military-procurement bribery scandals exposed in the summer 1988 could intensify pressures to cut the defense budget. But, even without such pressures, there is widespread public belief, shared by many business and political leaders and even former Defense Department officials, that the United States has been spending too lavishly and carelessly on military procurement and has been carrying too heavy a share of the defense burdens of the alliance.

During the Reagan military buildup, from 1981 through 1985, real military budget authority (corrected for inflation) grew by 53 percent, totaling over $1.4 trillion. The main recipient was weapons procurement, which more than doubled; this rush to procure doubtless did add to waste, fraud, and extravagance. The armed services rushed to commit funds; each branch drew up long shopping lists, which were not well coordinated. The result was that the military sought larger forces and modernization, not just with top-of-the-line existing weapons but for modernization with the next generation of ever more costly weapons; research, development, test, and evaluation spending authority rose by more than 80 percent.

The Army opted for a twenty-eight-division force, of which eighteen would be active duty and equipped with new tanks, new infantry fighting vehicles, new attack helicopters, and even a large fleet of new trucks. The Navy went for a 600-ship fleet, led by fifteen aircraft carrier battle groups (former Navy Secretary John Lehman wrote the contracts for three extra carrier groups in a way that would make it more costly to cancel than complete them), four reactivated battleships, and at least 100 nuclear attack submarines. The Air Force, competing with the Navy for the largest share of the budget, set out to modernize its strategic nuclear forces with two new bombers, upgraded B-52's, a new air-launched cruise missile, the MX intercontinental ballistic missile, and the small intercontinental ballistic missile known as the Midgetman, while also planning to increase its active and reserve fighter/attack wings and intercontinental airlift capacity.

The Pentagon was swamped with the task of managing so huge and costly a buildup. And, in the midst of all this, the president proposed the Strategic Defense Initiative, "Star Wars," the ultimate costs of which could run to hundreds of billions of dollars. With their relatively low start-up costs, the projects launched during the Reagan military buildup cast wedge-shaped shadows into the future, far exceeding the present or prospective resource capability of the existing tax structure.

The question is no longer whether to cut but where and how much. A reduction of U.S. military outlays from 6 percent to 5 percent of GNP, or 19 percent below its current path, would, as Mr. Brandon indicates, save $65 billion by 1993; but such a reduction would require not just canceling weapons or trimming force structures but also rearranging military and political alliances. Though the U.S. share of economic resources has declined in relation to that of its European allies and Japan, its military responsibilities have not been reduced proportionately. As a percentage of gross domestic product, the United States is carrying about twice the burden of the average of other NATO members. With the U.S. current account balance of payments in such deep deficit, this is a situation that cannot long continue.

Nevertheless, a reordering of defense responsibilities among the United States and its allies will doubtless mean extremely difficult and protracted negotiations, with significant differences among national military strategies and economic interests likely to produce clashes on many specific issues, such as weapons sales to NATO, trade relations, the provision of credits, and arms control and reduction agreements with the Soviet Union.

In my view, the most difficult problem facing the next American president will be how to scale back U.S. defense expenditures and commitments without jeopardizing its own security and without weakening the international defense and economic systems that have safeguarded world peace and prosperity for so long. There is urgent need for an integrated strategic plan that will foster both the economic and military security of the United States and its allies, in a new era.

If the resources that can be made available, by reducing wasteful or unnecessary expenditures in either the defense or social areas, are insufficient to enable the United States to fulfill its critical economic and military security requirements, then, as painful as it may be politically, taxes will have to be raised. The alternative of further weakening the economy or unduly cutting the nation's military and international obligations would be unacceptable—and dangerous.

Leonard Silk is economics columnist of the New York Times and distinguished professor of economics at Pace University. He was a member of the U.S. Mission to NATO and served on the Presidential Commission on Budget Concepts that recommended the unified budget under which the United States now operates.

Rimmer De Vries

On the Need for Higher U.S. Savings

No more urgent macroeconomic challenge confronts the next U.S. president and Congress than that of securing a major step-up in the nation's savings rate. Net savings sank below 2 percent of GNP in 1987, down from 5.5 percent at the beginning of the 1980s and less than one-quarter the savings effort achieved in the mid-1960s. Yet despite the dearth of saving, business investment surged higher in 1988 and real GNP growth ran at 3.5 percent or above—roughly the same pace as twenty years before. Why then is a big boost to saving so urgently needed?

Two reasons stand out. The first lies in the nation's external trade deficit—the direct manifestation of domestic saving deficiency relative to investment—which continues to run at an unsuitable magnitude. Though lower than in 1987, the red ink on merchandise trade for 1988 as a whole is likely to be around $130 billion, declining to about $100 billion in 1989. And the associated deficit on current account could add another $145 billion to U.S. net foreign liabilities, carrying it close to the half-trillion-dollar mark in the end of 1988; another $125 billion will probably be tacked on in 1989. That may not sound much of a burden on an economy generating a GNP of nearly $5 trillion, however, this perspective gives false comfort. The United States may not be headed for Latin America's agonies, but its foreign debt buildup heightens financial risk worldwide. Currency and capital markets everywhere are captivated and destabilized by the unprecedented absolute scale of the ongoing U.S. trade deficit and foreign debt accumulation.

The external imbalance is even more ominous in that it is a key determinant of national and international political perceptions of U.S. economic performance. The imbalance is seen as undermining the nation's global standing, as betokening incapacity to sustain *Pax Americana*, and as sounding the death knell for the relatively liberal trade and investment practices that have done so much to bind the free world nations together in uncommon prosperity since World War II.

The second reason to go for higher U.S. saving rests on the need to start positioning the U.S. economy now to cope with the strains that will arise once the baby-boom generation begins to retire early in the twenty-first century. The larger the nation's economic pie by that time, and the faster it continues to grow, the easier it should be to satisfy the working population while assuring retirees the increasing slice that their numbers and intergenerational equity will demand. Enlarging the pie is a matter of investing real resources both productively and in quantity. In order to achieve continuing increases in per-capita living standards for all, even as labor force growth stagnates, net investment in the U.S. economy needs to be on the order of 8 percent of GNP. In 1987, by contrast, net investment was a mere 5.3 percent of GNP and was two-thirds financed by net capital inflows from abroad. For both economic and political reasons, large-scale net foreign inflows can hardly be sustained through coming decades. Accordingly, in order to procure the resources for an adequate investment rate in the years ahead, the U.S. net savings rate, 1.9 percent of GNP in 1987, must quadruple.

How can this be accomplished? Saving was so slight in 1987 because the 5.3 percent of GNP collectively saved by the private sector and by state and local governments was largely offset by the federal government's dissaving of 3.4 percent of GNP via the budget deficit. Because postwar experience has shown little variation in the rate of private saving, it is not clear whether policies can be devised—regardless of political acceptability— that would be effective in raising private saving significantly.

With slim prospects for increased private saving, there is no alternative but to solve the shortfall in overall U.S. saving through an end to government dissaving. This is the fundamental rationale for steadfast implementation of the Gramm-Rudman-Hollings (GRH) budget targets during the next presidential term.

Unfortunately, temptations abound to fudge on GRH implementation. The latest temptation lies in the growing awareness of the burgeoning surplus of the social security system. That surplus, approximately $37 billion in fiscal year 1988, is projected to exceed almost $150 billion annually ten years hence.

All too many politicians and interest groups see the promise of surplus anywhere in the federal accounts as the signal for new spending schemes. In 1988, catastrophic health care insurance for the elderly was enacted and the Congress flirted with numerous other proposals for expanding medicare, notwithstanding its fast-rising outlays under current law and its projected deficits ten years from now. Just in time, the social security surplus offers itself as a natural cash cow for funding increased benefits for the elderly without having to grapple with the bloated costs and ineffective utilization containment now characterizing the U.S. health care system (the nation spends substantially more on health care in relation to GNP than do other industrial countries, yet to no better result as judged by aggregate health statistics).

Yet the social security surplus already is more than spoken for during the four years of the next administration. The increase in the surplus through fiscal year 1993 alone should provide almost half of the $150 billion reduction in the federal budget deficit (unified definition) that GRH supposedly mandates. If the social security surplus is tapped for other uses, either tax increases and cuts in on-line budget items will have to be correspondingly more savage or the budget deficit reduction targets will wind up on the scrap heap.

Taking the latter course—which is, naturally, the politically easy one—would be a grave error. The twin deficit connection cannot be wished away: failure to eliminate the budget deficit on the GRH schedule would prolong the trade deficit and compound its risks, not least that of making reality of the fashionable prophecies of inexorable U.S. decline.

Instead, the social security surplus needs to be preserved as part of a balanced and credible fiscal package to meet the GRH targets. Ideally, such a package would shift resources toward capital formation and away from consumption, by relying principally on consumption taxes—on gasoline, for example—plus further cuts in consumption-subsidizing expenditures. To be politically viable, however, a fiscal package will have to be carefully crafted both to elicit sacrifice from all segments of society yet also to meet diverse economic and social concerns.

That will be no small undertaking. Still, the pain involved is overstated if viewed exclusively through fiscal spectacles. What should not be overlooked is the scope for easier monetary policy that decisive fiscal action would provide, indeed would require to maintain full employment. The appropriate monetary offset would allow reasonably noninflationary growth to go forward and would open the way to some further downward correction of the dollar's exchange value. Though depreciation would be premature right now, it would be constructive in healing the trade deficit once fiscal action frees up the necessary resources.

So too would be success in maintaining the faster growth of the global economy that has been the major positive surprise of the past twelve months. Cooperation among the Group of Five countries can be valuable to this end as a means to exchange ideas and information and to enhance understanding. Cooperation, however, is no substitute for the difficult domestic choices necessary to resolve the key imbalances.

The United States has to come to terms with the reality that sustained trade adjustment entails domestic consumption restraint. That does not necessarily imply an outright reduction in U.S. living standards. Rather, fiscal discipline to restrain consumption is the tested road to increased saving and investment, and, in turn the foundation for higher living standards in years to come.

If the next president and Congress take the road of fiscal probity, U.S. standing will rise around the world. Other major trading nations—notably the Europeans, still plagued by horrendous unemployment—will better see their self-interest in rooting prosperity firmly on supply-side dynamism and domestic sources of growth. Developing countries would benefit by lower interest rates and healthier and more diversified export markets. None of these objectives need be hostage to the day that some grand international monetary reform can be gotten off the ground. Instead, U.S. leadership and initiative are all that is needed for lift-off.

Rimmer De Vries is currently senior vice president and chief economist of Morgan Guaranty Trust Company, and editor of its publication World Financial Markets.

Lawrence A. Veit

On the Case Against Excessive Pessimism

History will recall 1987 as the year when an increasingly fragile U.S. economy was undermined by currency instability to the point that the stock market crashed. Confidence in the equity market ebbed throughout the summer, progressively weakened by the sustained erosion of the dollar and the related fall of bond prices. Behind this decay stood a rising pessimism about America's ability to narrow its federal budget and foreign trade deficits. The gloom deepened as a variety of other problems gained prominence, mainly recurrent fears of inflation, excessive domestic and external indebtedness, protectionism, oil price volatility, and armed conflict in the Middle East.

Contrast the 1987 panic and its underlying causes with the actual performance of the U.S. economy, however, and a more complex, less one-sided reality emerges. In 1987, U.S. output expanded 2.9 percent, 3.1 million new jobs were created, and the rate of consumer price inflation was held to 3.6 percent. Not only was the world economy moderately prosperous in 1987, but a base was established for sustaining the good times in 1988 and future years. And, as the linkage between the United States and other economies grew, the need for Washington to give high priority to international economic policy also increased.

Optimists and pessimists today agree that the U.S. economy is vulnerable to shocks. They differ sharply, however, regarding: (1) the relationship between the "twin" budget and trade deficits; (2) the dollar exchange rate that would be most desirable; and (3) whether the United States should act individually or in concert with its trade partners to resolve mutual problems. At the heart of the controversy are contrary understandings of how the economy operates. In particular, opinions differ regarding the costs of the dollar's overvaluation in the first half of the 1980s, as well as how much time will be required for the subsequent dollar depreciation to undo the large imbalances.

In this context, one must reconsider the twin deficits. An important causal link exists between the budget and trade, but the idea that there is a one-to-one relationship is ill considered. All the governments of the world cumulatively have a budget deficit. In contrast, the cumulative global trade and current accounts must, by definition, equal zero. Indeed, Japan, Germany, and many other nations simultaneously record budget deficits and trade surpluses. Thus, part of the U.S. problem is that when the federal deficit was increased in the early 1980s, there was no offsetting policy to raise domestic private savings. Foreign savings filled the gap, and the flood of incoming capital initially pushed the dollar to unreasonable heights.

Most observers agree that direct measures to reduce the federal deficit will also improve the external position. The reverse process, often overlooked, is equally important—measures to eliminate the U.S. trade deficit will, by creating income and savings, also reduce the budget deficit. Thus, direct actions by the next administration to reduce the budget deficit should share priority with a liberal, pro-active trade policy and with efforts to stabilize the dollar's exchange rate at a competitive level. (For example, the need to address trade issues independently is demonstrated by studies which document that Europe and Japan subsidize their agriculture far more than the United States.)

While acknowledging the urgency of action to reduce the federal deficit, the timing and amount needed—and the implied pain—are often overstated, given the large size of the U.S. gross national product (roughly $4.5 trillion). Any combination of spending reduction and new revenues equivalent to one percent of GNP would be worth roughly $45 billion, probably more when credit is taken for the accompanying benefits of lower interest rates. Too little attention is paid to the fact that the deficit has already been cut from $221.2 billion in fiscal year 1986 to $150.4 billion in 1987. The fall is even sharper if measured as a percent of GNP. Nor is enough attention paid to the budget surplus of state and local governments, which amounts to approximately $50 billion. Finally, cynics dismiss the National Economic Commission appointed by President Reagan to deal with the federal deficit without reflecting on how, a decade earlier, a similar commission, chaired by Alan Greenspan, resolved the problem of the social security system's potential insolvency. In short, action to reduce the federal deficit is urgent, but if real GNP growth can be maintained at moderate levels in the next several years, the federal budget issue may recede remarkably fast.

The case for dollar depreciation to levels below those reached early in 1988 rests on the presumption that high import prices could reduce domestic purchasing power—curtailing consumer demand—and that this is needed to spur a major gain in net exports. The contrary case is based on the power of further dollar depreciation to cause havoc by: (1) igniting an inflationary binge that would bring Federal Reserve tightening and recession; (2) causing a more pronounced repeat of the financial panic of 1987, or (3) inducing protectionism and a trade war. Looking at recent data, further dollar depreciation seems not only risky, but unnecessary. In inflation-adjusted terms, the U.S. trade deficit has improved in five of the past six quarters, from $47.2 billion in the third quarter of 1986 to $36.7 billion in the first quarter of 1988. The cascading dollar has delayed improvement in the nominal trade deficit by causing import prices to rise faster than export prices. Currently, however, the value of exports is rising four times faster than that of imports and a $35 billion improvement seems likely in 1988. Productivity and unit-labor-cost statistics all point to a further reduction in the trade deficit in 1989.

The most overlooked positive factor for the U.S. economy is a flood of foreign direct investment that is rapidly transforming weakness into strength. Almost every prominent foreign manufacturing company is currently establishing production facilities in the United States—transferring technology, creating jobs, and increasing industrial capacity. U.S. firms are responding with their own plant and equipment spending, and the probability is growing that the U.S. economy will be strengthened dramatically by this investment, just as the European "economic miracle" was largely due to the combination of U.S. and domestic European investment in the 1950s and 1960s. The automobile industry is the most obvious case where rising domestic U.S. production by Japanese-owned firms is substituting for imports; with Japan holding a constant share of a flat market, more than 400,000 vehicles may be affected in the brief 1987–89 period. From a macroeconomic point of view, the $42 billion inflow of foreign direct investment that arrived in 1987 may result in $80 billion additional production in 1988 and in future years, a significant amount even in a $4.5 trillion economy. U.S. companies have responded with accelerated plant and equipment spending that will further improve America's position.

An important difference between the budget and trade deficits is that when government IOUs are held by domestic persons and institutions they have less adverse impact than when they are held by foreigners. Witness the success of Japan, Germany, and other "profligate" nations which, despite large government debt, continue to be regarded as sound because they have international creditor status. Accordingly, the next president should concentrate on reduction of the federal deficit, but not to the exclusion of efforts to get rid of the trade imbalance. Policies to increase the U.S. private savings rate, given the European and Japanese experience, should be regarded as a viable alternative to reducing the deficit.

To sum up, we protest too much! Our economy is prosperous and imbalances are being reduced. For the next president, a successful economic policy will require a blend of current policies and new measures. A total shift in policy would be as destructive as staying the current course. Urgent attention should be devoted to a multipronged initiative with the following major elements:

- Create stable expectations for consumers, the business community, and financial markets. This will require a reasonably stable dollar and a policy that places increased reliance on fiscal responsibility to curb inflation. A smaller budget deficit would relieve the Federal Reserve from having to act strenuously to raise interest rates and tighten liquidity.
- Specifically, enact modest actions to gradually increase budget revenues. Excise taxes appear to offer scope for reducing the federal deficit without, at the same time, destroying incentives or being too regressive. In particular, a value-added tax could provide revenue, enhance the honesty of the tax system, and also provide some support for the U.S. foreign trade position.
- Protectionism may be the ultimate alternative to a trade policy that fails to provide legitimate protection to U.S. business in the face of foreign dumping, subsidies, and less-than-open markets. Thus, judicious use should be made of the president's negotiating authority and his power to get tough when U.S. business is being treated shoddily abroad.

Recent data indicate that the U.S. economy is responding to existing policies. Bearing in mind that economic adjustment is a process, not an event, the next president should formulate new measures with an understanding that he must allow time for the competitive advantages of past dollar devaluation and foreign direct investment to have an impact on the system. Whereas international cooperation can rarely substitute for good domestic policy, it should be easy to recognize that nations have mutual interests, and that these and more purely domestic goals can best be achieved in an environment of cooperation. If our economic interdependence is ignored, we are bound to lose economic opportunities and incur excessive geopolitical costs.

Lawrence A. Veit is manager and international economist at Brown Brothers Harriman & Company. Previously, he was with the U.S. Treasury, the State Department and the Conference Board.

William D. Eberle

On U.S. Trade Policy

Successful U.S. participation in the international trade and investment system is critical to our standard of living. U.S. policy toward trade is important in itself, but such policy and practice will be effective only if the United States has a sound basis for its domestic economic policy.

The next president must have a clear understanding that *if* the administration and Congress fail to restore fiscal responsibility and end our reliance upon borrowing foreign capital, *if* the major industrial nations fail to better coordinate their macroeconomic policies, *if* these countries fail to maintain realistically aligned and reasonably stable exchange rates, and *if* they fail to restore capital flows to developing countries and enable them to grow, U.S. trade performance will suffer and no trade policy can compensate. The savings/investment balance, relative rates of growth in the United States and abroad, and exchange rates will all then have a greater impact on trade performance than will trade policy.

Nevertheless, trade policy is vitally important. By determining the conditions of access for foreign goods to the American market, by setting U.S. goals for increasing market access overseas, and by exercising leadership to expand world trade, trade policy can go a long way toward both improving U.S. economic welfare and stimulating domestic and world growth.

The new president will inherit a trade policy "ledger" with substantial assets and liabilities. U.S. manufacturers are in a strong competitive position thanks to realistic exchange rates and significant gains in productivity in recent years. The United States is still running an unacceptably high trade deficit, however, and our rapidly accumulating external debt may exceed $550 billion on Inauguration Day. To service and ultimately repay this debt, an open trading system and healthy world growth will be essential.

The next president inherits two major liabilities which he must overcome. One is skepticism in Congress and the private sector over the management of trade policy by all presidents. This traditional skepticism grew dramatically during the high dollar Reagan years. The next president must take advantage of his "honeymoon" to launch initiatives that will enable him to stay on the "offensive," while building confidence in his management of trade policy. The other liability is the serious erosion of U.S. leadership enjoyed for the past forty years. The world desperately needs economic leadership, however, and no one else has the ability and the willingness to provide it. Exercising leadership in these circumstances will require great effort and skill.

The next president must have a clear and publicly stated policy, and a single designated cabinet member as point person. He must recognize trade as a national priority. In order to accomplish this, he must obtain a *congressional mandate* so that all policy and legislation takes into account the impact on competitiveness and exports, and he must *set the tone* with a clear and early statement of his trade policy.

More specifically, the next president should:

- Recognize trade as an important national priority, reflecting its importance to the economy, consistently in rhetoric and in appointments.
- Extol the benefits that competition through trade provides, especially the stimulus to excellence from which both consumers and producers gain.
- Work with Congress to mandate that all legislation addresses the impact on competitiveness and trade.
- Inform trading partners that the United States expects them to join with us in strengthening international discipline over trade. Advise them that the United States will not tolerate mercantilist, advocating, or protectionist policies and will act

forcefully, within the context of international obligations, against them.

- To ensure effective development and execution of trade policy, to send a signal to our trading partners that the United States "means business," and to help restore confidence in Congress and the private sector, the president should clearly delegate responsibility and authority for the conduct of trade policy. This does not necessarily mean creating a cabinet department for trade; reorganization proposals too often substitute for sound policy prescriptions. What it does mean is: (1) designating a single cabinet officer with lead responsibility for all domestic and international economic affairs, including trade and (2) organizing all aspects of international economic policy.

- Reinvigorate the Uruguay Round by making the 1990 deadline for a successful conclusion of the negotiations—to strengthen the discipline of international rules, and to expand the coverage of those rules to new arenas of commerce—a top priority of the first term. Make clear that multilateral trade liberalization is the preferred U.S. approach, but make equally clear that the United States will not permit progress to be held hostage to a "least common denominator" and that it will actively explore plurilateral alternatives.

- Announce a program of prompt and practical enforcement of U.S. trade laws.

- Announce a program of action within a set time frame to continue to improve U.S. competitiveness through: (1) a removal of export restraints; (2) reinvigorated export promotion; and (3) a program of changes in tax law to encourage competitiveness, such as credit, consumption tax, and assistance to education.

- Resist simplistic formulas or "wholesale" solutions to trade problems and be wary of pleas for fairness that disguise campaigns for protection. Endure some frustration over the slow process of international negotiations and the seemingly unending series of product conflicts that will arise, but set firm deadlines to settle disputes and then act.

• Strive for better international economic coordination. Keep pressure on surplus countries to accept responsibility to adjust. Keep pressure on newly industrializing countries to abandon mercantilist trade policies, which depend on foreign demand rather than domestic demand for growth. Promote multilateral surveillance to keep international "heat" on countries failing to pull their weight.

Adoption of such a balanced approach by the next president will allow exports to grow to bring the trade deficit into surplus, and world growth to continue so that adjustments can be made successfully.

William D. Eberle was the U.S. Special Trade Representative from 1971 to 1975, and is currently chairman of Manchester Associates, Ltd., an international consulting firm.

Murray H. Finley

On the Human Concerns

January 1989 marks the end of the administration of President Reagan. In 1988, unemployment was 5.3 percent, and some 14 million to 15 million new jobs have been created since 1980. Although the global economy has changed dramatically in the past decade, the massive tax cuts of the Reagan years and the deregulation of industry and the financial markets have unleashed the free market and, with the help of the "invisible hand" of Adam Smith, the administration that follows has but to "stay the course." Or does it?

The official unemployment rate counts as employed, all those who work one hour or more during the survey week each month; all those who actively, but unsuccessfully, looked for work during the previous four weeks are counted as unemployed. However, if the unemployed figure takes into account both discouraged workers who have dropped out of the labor market and involuntary part-time workers, the "real" jobless figure becomes sadly very different. The unemployment rate, in fact, rose from 7.9 percent in 1979 to 11.5 percent in 1987.

From 1975 to 1980, 2.7 million new jobs per year were added to the economy. Contrast that to the 2 million added from 1980 to 1987. In other words, new jobs were added 30 percent more slowly in the 1980s than in the 1970s. Furthermore, real income, in terms of hourly rates, has fallen to the earnings level of 1970. Moreover, the percentage of Americans living in poverty was 13.6 percent in 1986, which is a 2.5 percent increase from the 1973 level. And worst of all, one-fifth of the children in the United States now live in poverty.

Recently, the Council on Competitiveness published its first competitiveness index, which compares current U.S. performance to that of the past and to that of other nations. The index measured U.S. growth of standard of living, trade, productivity, and investment, and compared them to average growth of the other seven summit nations. In all four categories, the study concluded that, since 1972, the United States has not kept pace with the performance of our major foreign competitors.

During the Reagan years, the overall tax burden on the lower 20 percent of our population increased, while that of the upper 20 percent declined. There has been, in effect, a redistribution of income—taking from the poorest in our society and giving to the most affluent.

The cuts in personal marginal rates and corporate taxation were intended to spur productive investment. However, since 1980, the share of fixed investment in GNP has fallen from 19.1 percent to 16.1 percent in the United States. Companies are using profits for investment in purely financial assets, with the focus on short-term return. This trend has been aggravated by the flurry of predatory takeovers and the threat of the same.

Finally, the public investment needed to maintain our infrastructure has dwindled. The deterioration of our highways and bridges is approaching emergency proportions. Our mass transit systems are incapable of transporting our people. Our housing stock, particularly in the inner cities, is a disgrace. And our sewage, waste disposal, and water supply systems are increasingly inadequate.

Yet, having said all of the above, in some aspects, our record surpasses those of other nations. Unemployment has grown in Western Europe in each of the past seventeen years. Third World per-capita GNP is now below its peak of ten years ago. The United States, in contrast, has had six years of GNP growth. What has been the secret of our success? The answer lies in but a few words: spend substantially more than your income, consume more than you produce, and borrow the billions and billions necessary to produce this "economic miracle." The Reagan administration increased the federal debt by more than the total debt accumulated by all previous administrations since the adoption of our Constitution. When President Reagan took office in 1981, the United States was the largest creditor nation on earth. As he leaves office, seven and one-half years later, we are the largest debtor country, with a foreign indebtedness of almost $400 billion, financed by massive foreign investments from Japan, Canada, Europe, the oil-producing countries, and so forth.

The new administration will inherit a tremendous federal deficit, an equally tremendous trade deficit, a Third World debt that threatens the economic and political stability of many of these countries and equally jeopardizes our financial system, a steadily reducing competitive position vis-à-vis our major competitors, and a growing underclass in the United States. So, perhaps, we may have to modify our course somewhat.

If we are going to compete effectively in the global economy, we will have to stop wasting our human resources. It is estimated that 700,000 American children drop out of high school each year, and another 700,000 graduate but cannot read their diplomas. Our educational system needs a major repairing, with headstart programs, child care for children of working parents, remedial education, decent equipment, classrooms, and schools, and higher-paid and better-trained teachers, all of which requires massive expenditures of federal funds.

An adequate adjustment assistance program should be instituted to help workers dislocated as a result of plant closings or massive layoffs. The program should provide retraining and relocation if necessary. Besides the social and human misery caused by unemployment, the Congressional Budget Office, in a

1986 study, concluded that each percentage point of excess unemployment costs the United States $44 billion in lost tax revenues and payments for unemployment compensation and other social benefit programs.

The next administration will have to address the need to encourage productive and job-creating investment. Specific measures, including taxation, should be reintroduced to discourage speculative activity in order to make it less profitable than real investment.

Massive public investment to rebuild our infrastructure is vital and urgently needed. Many of the areas would involve joint public and private sector activity.

The massive debt owed by most of the developing countries creates the potential for increased instability in those countries, and diminished opportunities for international trade. The loss of stock market values, following the October 19, 1987, crash, was greater than the total indebtedness of all developing countries. These losses have been absorbed with relatively little complaint, while proposals for debt write-offs or interest relief are dismissed. To propose that these countries tighten their belts even further, reduce consumption and increase exports to facilitate debt repayment, is shifting the burden from the lenders onto the already impoverished workers of the developing countries, as well as onto the American workers who would pay the cost through loss of jobs from such increased exports to the United States. Partial debt write-offs and reduced interest payments are necessary so as not to further jeopardize economic and social programs in the developing countries. Can one imagine the consequences to the United States if Mexico's already fragile economy, with extremely high unemployment, deteriorates further? If this were to happen, the cost to the United States, in terms of economic aid, and who knows, military preparedness, would make Mexico's $100 billion debt pale to insignificance.

Prior to the Reagan years, our system helped to decrease the number of people at the lowest income level, and the promise of a rise up the economic ladder has been a driving force in our economy. The system enabled U.S. workers to make enough money to buy the goods produced. The reverse is the situation in a major portion of the developing world. The maldistribution of income inhibits not only social progress but the ability to develop growth and markets. South Korea is an interesting case study. With the recent development towards greater political democracy has come the inevitable growth of free democratic trade unions in South Korea. The recent strikes there, considering the years of repression in trade union rights, have been surprisingly short-lived and relatively peaceful. Yet, the workers, as a consequence, have made substantial economic gains. Korean workers will be able to purchase the cars and other products they produce so capably. This should ease their export-driven economy, and make possible further opening of their market for goods manufactured in the United States and elsewhere. Democracy has birth pangs, but the benefits in economic and social programs are so self-evident that we should encourage the free-association of workers as one of the key elements in promoting growth domestically and internationally.

Unfortunately, too many governments permit violations of internationally agreed-upon worker and trade union rights and minimum labor standards, in order to capture export markets and to attract foreign investment. The benefit of growing international trade is to increase social and economic progress, to contribute to rising standards of living. To further this fundamental aim, a social clause embodying workers' rights must be included in the GATT, and any violation should be expressly designated as an unfair trading practice.

The international trading system, established under GATT after the World War II, operated reasonably well for a number of decades. But it was never intended to cope with the massive unemployment, slow or even negative growth, and volatile exchange rate changes of the past fifteen years. The use of subsidies, the denial of workers' rights, dumping, tariff and nontariff barriers to trade, the failure to recognize the importance of social aspects of trade, all have endangered the multilateral trading system. Unless these problems and principles are successfully addressed, the ongoing trade talks—the Uruguay Round—will not retard the break-up of the multilateral trading system. Coordination with our major trading partners, both the industrial and developing ones, though extremely difficult, is, nevertheless, vital if the Uruguay Round is to be a success.

The Reagan years, predicated on the belief that an unencumbered and unregulated market would create wealth and opportunities for all, are coming to an end. The next administration, if it hopes to begin solving the problems it has inherited, will have to return to the philosophy that government has an important and vital role to play in approaching our domestic shortcomings, and to begin to confront the changed global economy.

Murray H. Finley is the Rust visiting professor at the Darden Graduate School of Business Administration, University of Virginia; chairman of the Advisory Committee of the Amalgamated Bank of New York; and president emeritus of the Amalgamated Clothing and Textile Workers Union.

John R. Petty

On U.S. Development Assistance

If at any point in time politics and economics may be viewed separately, their interactions over a period of time become a blend. In his recent well-publicized book, *The Rise and Fall of the Great Powers*, Professor Paul Kennedy reminds us of this lesson of history even if his current applications seem somewhat stretched.

Pursuit of the U.S. national interest internationally has economic and financial dimensions just as it does political. Moreover, just as the postwar U.S. political hegemony has diminished and altered, so too has unrivaled U.S. economic leadership waned.

Yet, we as a nation have not fully adapted to the implications this reality should have upon our conduct of affairs abroad. Politically, our leadership role is now more shared: our posture today is more that of a chairman of the board than that of the commander in chief. While it is commonplace to speak of the globalization of our markets and the economic interdependence of nations, we are less quick to consider the implications these realities have upon the manner in which we pursue our interests. Nowhere is this transformation more relevant than in our financial and economic affairs.

Encouraging economic development in the developing countries has long been an important national interest of the United States. However, bilateral economic assistance dedicated to this broad mission is inadequately funded (special cases aside), and the prospects are dim for any significant reversal of this pattern. In times past, bilateral aid has been an important means both of demonstrating our interest and concern in reducing poverty, and of fostering investment and growth in needy economies. Helping these countries achieve significant economic progress remains strongly in the U.S. interest. Economic growth is necessary to assist the young democratic societies meet the needs of their people. Favorable prospects for economic growth foster free and pluralistic societies, which, in turn, are the most promising environment for raising standards of living.

While bilateral aid remains an important tool of U.S. national policy, it is through the multilateral development institutions like the World Bank, the Inter-American Development Bank, and other regional banks where the greatest economic leverage can be achieved. These multilateral institutions provide both the most efficient use of U.S. aid resources, and the best means of mobilizing the funds necessary to further global development ambitions. These institutions also play a critical role with respect to the two issues which now dominate development assistance. One concerns the very poor, another, the not so poor.

The Black African countries fall into the first category, the very poor. It is here that humanitarian concerns are predominant, but economy building cannot be far behind. Primarily grant assistance is required, as the recent Mitterand plan for donor governments to cancel one-third of past loans to Africa demonstrates. Responding to this urgent need will be difficult and frustrating to the new administration. Available resources will be disappointingly small for these very poor nations—especially grant money which is best suited for their stage of development. A determined cooperative effort, perhaps under the leadership of the United Nations and no doubt with the large support of members of the European Community, should be pursued.

Regarding the not so poor, the problem of the debt burden of the middle-income developing countries, primarily in Latin America, is entering a new phase. It is maturing now to the point where a more activist posture is called for from the new administration. While the possibility of the debt problem becoming unraveled has not disappeared, circumstances provide an opportunity of our meaningfully influencing events.

"Muddling through" was the only practical alternative in the past, but, in the future, higher ambitions for growth should be pursued. Economic reform and modernization of these mostly Latin American economies is the only lasting path to sustained growth. Policies designed to encourage political leaders in the borrower countries to pursue the course of modernization energetically will best serve their long-term interests. Subsidies and protection offer no enduring hope to Latin American competitiveness in the global economy. A delayed response to the opportunity will be expensive. Active U.S. financial leadership (frequently exercised behind the scene) oriented toward selectively and prudently marshalling and coordinating the players in the debt crisis to address the circumstances of each particular country is required. Our efforts should seek to encourage a constructive domestic program by borrowers, with concessions from lenders, which works to help assure positive results of new programs. Rewards may be more constructive than inducements.

The promise of success is better than is usually thought. The opportunities to raise growth to a level supportive of more extensive reforms are real. Major sums of official funds are not in the cards. Rather a more flexible and active use of the tools and resources available, and the active leadership role of the United States, is what is necessary.

Exercising financial and economic leadership in the present environment is essential to pursue our national interests. Our new style must be reflective of a more shared leadership and exercised as appropriate through multilateral bodies where our special role is recognized, but the merits of our positions must be argued and explained with knowledge and skill. The give and take of this mutual process—including incorporating positive aspects contributed by others—is our best means to assure timely and effective action with the maximum of resources directed toward an important and solvable problem.

In summary, the new administration has a unique opportunity to provide financial and economic leadership in the development process—fully reinforcing to our political objectives—on a range of critical and solvable issues in nearby countries of long-term importance to us.

The nature of this leadership must reflect the evolving global scene; it must be shared, but not less dynamic.

As a stimulator and coordinator, the United States has a vital role to play. The new president will sometimes appear as a chairman of the board who must work through an independent but generally supportive committee. Our economic and political interests can be served in a manner reaffirming U.S. leadership, responding to the opportunity and reflective of the new circumstances in which we must act.

John R. Petty is currently the chairman of the High-Level Review Committee of the Inter-American Development Bank, which is charged with redefining the role of the Bank for the 1990s. He is the retired chairman of Marine Midland Banks, Inc.

Bruce Stokes

On Technology and Economic Policymaking

When the Economic Policy Council or its equivalent sits down for its first meeting in the next administration, the new president's most important economic advisor will not even be in the room. Assembled around the table will be, among others, the Treasury secretary, the Commerce secretary, and the U.S. trade representative. If precedent holds any weight in the future, however, the president's science advisor will not have been invited.

With the United States and the world in the midst of the most important technological revolution since the eighteenth century, pigeonholing the science advisor would be a grievous error. For, in the years ahead, it will be science and technology policy, not monetary and fiscal policy, that is likely to have the greatest influence on the long-term health of the U.S. economy and the international competitiveness of American industry. And if the next president disregards this fact, it will be at the economy's risk.

For politicians and presidents, science and technology have long been exotic topics, grist for inspirational speeches about space travel or "Star Wars" missile defense. For economists, they have been immutable givens, not relevant to day-to-day policy-making.

But all that is changing. New technologies—on the shop floor, on the farm, and in the laboratory—are the foundation of the new economy, and technological innovation is happening so rapidly that it is driving rather than following policymaking.

For example, in recent years, while policymakers dithered over the decline of American manufacturing and, more recently, breathed a sigh of relief as it has rebounded due to the falling value of the dollar, they have all but ignored new developments *inside* the manufacturing sector. There, the long-term evolution-ary development of industrial technology has become a revolu-tion through the introduction of computer-integrated, robot-driven, flexible manufacturing technologies and techniques that permit rapid adaptation to the constantly fluctuating interna-tional business environment.

In this environment, new technologies are minimizing the impact of many macroeconomic policies, such as changes in the exchange rate. They are altering long-standing rules of the game, such as the dumping code. And, in the long run, flexible manufacturing may profoundly affect trade flows themselves.

With these consequences already apparent, failure to integrate an understanding of new developments in science and technolo-gy into economic policymaking could doom the next president to decisions that are rapidly overtaken by events.

We are in the midst of the second industrial revolution. Industrial automation has been going on for a generation. In the last decade, however, it has shifted into overdrive. In more and more factories, computers are being married to multipurpose, reprogrammable machine tools, robots, lasers, and new techniques for pre-forming and shaping materials. These technologies permit large production runs for small numbers of separate products, with the changeover taking place at the touch of a button. As a result, labor costs are almost nonexistent. At the margin, production costs are minimized. And, because production can be so rapidly adjusted to match changing consumer tastes, the manufacturer's proximity to the market is of overwhelming importance.

The policy implications of this technological revolution are already becoming apparent. The Reagan administration's lack of technological sophistication led it to badly underestimate the ability of the Japanese economy and its producers to adapt to the recent rapid appreciation of the yen.

Lowering the value of the dollar was supposed to reduce U.S. imports from Japan by making Japanese goods more expensive. But it took nearly three years for this to happen. Why? In part because Japanese companies, who outspent U.S. firms two to one in automation from 1981 to 1986, were able to cut their production costs even faster than the decline in the dollar. As a result, while the dollar was worth 132 yen in early August 1988, Matsushita Electric Company (which owns the Panasonic label) estimates that it can operate profitably anywhere above 57 yen to the dollar; Hitachi claims its breakeven point is 93 yen to the dollar; and NEC Corporation's is 110.

Since no one has ever suggested allowing the dollar to slide to those lows, one policy implication of flexible manufacturing is to limit the effectiveness of exchange rate changes in redressing trade imbalances. Macroeconomists in future Treasury Departments should take note.

In the future, flexible manufacturing may also bestow similar trade benefits on the United States. For example, component fabrication in electronics manufacturing, which is 25 percent automated today, is expected to be 80 percent automated in the early 1990s. At that level of automation, there will be little need for U.S. electronics manufacturers to seek out low-cost overseas labor. And much of their production may return to the United

States to reduce transportation costs and management problems. Protectionist policies formulated today, with no vision of how manufacturing technology could reverse trade flows in the future, could well limit future U.S. export potential.

Similarly, the future spread of flexible manufacturing technology among small manufacturers is likely to strengthen that traditionally important sector of the American economy, dramatically improving U.S. competitiveness in the 1990s. Much of that potential benefit may be lost, however, if the small-manufacturing sector is allowed to continue to shrink at its current pace.

To avoid these and similar problems, and to adequately integrate an appreciation for new developments in science and technology into economic policymaking, will not be easy. Any new administration will have to proceed along several fronts at once.

A new president would do well to beef up existing Commerce Department efforts to encourage manufacturers to adopt advanced manufacturing processes. The Defense Department already has an extensive program with this goal in conjunction with defense contractors. There is no reason why such initiatives should be limited to the defense industrial base, especially since economic security issues rather than strategic ones are likely to preoccupy policymakers in the years ahead.

The now extinct investment tax credit stimulated an estimated $80 billion in automation investments. It might be useful to resurrect the credit, and, in the interest of revenue saving, to target it solely on productivity-enhancing investments.

The looming national debate on foreign investment might be focused, as much as possible, on issues of technology transfer, not ownership per se. Many Japanese companies are not utilizing their most advanced manufacturing processes in their American facilities, minimizing the spin-off benefits for the U.S. economy. European experience suggests that requiring such investors to transfer their latest technology to their foreign subsidiaries could prove beneficial.

Regulatory reform is also in order to ensure that accounting procedures, antitrust regulations, and so forth encourage investment in new technologies and cooperation among those who develop and use new manufacturing techniques.

In addition, in the current round of multilateral trade negotiations, the new president would do well to follow the Reagan administration's lead and focus on removing foreign trade barriers, to open the way for the expected boom in U.S. manufactured exports, and to liberalize trade in services especially for items like computer programs for machine tools.

At the same time, the economic policy response to new technological developments will involve what to avoid as much as what to do. In the eight years of the Reagan administration, import restraints were used to protect the automobile, steel, and other industries. The problems were real, but the solutions were static, freezing the industries in place.

In the future, politically inevitable protection for important producers should have a price—adjustment through adoption of advanced manufacturing techniques. The Pentagon, hoping to improve quality and lower costs, is already using the threat of the loss of government contracts to force its suppliers to introduce flexible manufacturing. There is no reason why similar leverage should not be applied to improve U.S. international competitiveness in key industries.

These and similar policies dealing with biotechnologies, new materials technologies, and advanced electronics will be critical for any American president hoping to fashion regulatory, trade, fiscal, and monetary policies to deal with the evolving U.S. economy.

Beyond specific policies, the next president will also need to project a vision in all that he does that reflects an understanding that the future will not be like the past. This may be the toughest challenge of all, both politically and bureaucratically. Policymaking is easiest when there are few discontinuities with what went before. And few leaders have gone wrong basing their policies and betting their political futures on traditional thinking. Unless, of course, they were the political leaders of the mid-eighteenth century, many of whom cast their fate with agriculture rather than with the new-fangled spinning looms and steam engines. They might advise the next president to include that science advisor in economic policy meetings.

Bruce Stokes is the international economics correspondent for the National Journal. He was director of outreach at the Worldwatch Institute and an associate producer of National Public Radio's "All Things Considered."

The Steering Committee
The Council on Foreign Relations International Trade Project

Edmund T. Pratt, Jr., *Chairman*
C. Michael Aho, *Director of Project*
Suzanne H. Hooper, *Assistant Director of Project*

Members, The Study Group on
the Economic Choices Confronting the Next President

Anthony M. Solomon, *Chairman*
C. Michael Aho, *Study Group Director*
Stephanie E. Hoelscher, *Rapporteur*

Roger C. Altman
C. Fred Bergsten
Richard Brandon
Sam Y. Cross
Kenneth W. Dam
Richard G. Darman
Rimmer De Vries
William Dewald
William Diebold, Jr.
William D. Eberle
Thomas Ostrom Enders
Richard D. Erb
Martin S. Feldstein
Steven Fenster
Murray H. Finley
Ellen L. Frost
Richard N. Gardner
William H. Gleysteen, Jr.
George J.W. Goodman
Victor Gotbaum

Sylvia Ann Hewlett
Richard C. Holbrooke
Karen Elliot House
Shafiqul Islam
Henry Kaufman
Roger M. Kubarych
Marc Levinson
Carol O'Cleireacain
Peter G. Peterson
John R. Petty
Daniel A. Sharp
Leonard Silk
Edson W. Spenser
Joan E. Spero
David Stockman
Alan Stoga
Bruce Stokes
Peter Tarnoff
Lawrence A. Veit
Marina v.N. Whitman

Index

Adjustment, domestic: *See* Labor adjustment

Africa, 65–66, 70, 75

African Development Bank, 70

Agency for International Development, 77

Agriculture, 18, 73, 90, 104, 108, 109, 110–11; decoupling subsidies from U.S. production, 110, 111; domestic support programs, 108, 110–11, 178; European Community, 85–86, 92, 106, 108, 111; next president's approach to reducing subsidies in, 109–11; subsidies, 18, 30, 106, 108–11; surplus capacity, 104; U.S. competitiveness in, 110, 111; in Uruguay Round, 89–90, 91–92

Agriculture Foreign Investment Disclosure Act, 164

Anchor approach, 52; *see also* Exchange rates

Antitrust law, U.S., 119, 152

Apparel industry: promotion of automation in, 117–18; versus textiles, 116; *see also* Textiles and apparel

Asian Development Bank, 70

Australia, 108, 109, 164

Automobiles, 46, 85, 114, 119, 161, 163, 166, 167

Baker, James A. III, 65, 84, 182–83

Baker Plan, 65

Balance of payments, 63, 70, 72, 73

Baldrige, Malcolm, 170

Bank of International Settlements, 146–47, 179; *see also* International economic institutions

Banks, banking, 4, 5–6, 16–17, 68, 167; agreement on minimum capital standards for, 145–48; consolidated supervision of, 143–44; currency trading by, 47–48; differing national traditions in, 141, 145; European Community, 145, 147, 153–55; European licenses for, 153–54, harmonization of rules for, 16–17, 143, 148, 179; international agreements on, 147–48; international regulation of, 143–48, Japanese, 145–46,

166–67; nonlending activities of, 145–46; reasons for international rules on, 145–46; spread of activity across national borders, 141–42, 145; trade-related questions of, 143; U.S. regulations of, 68–69, 145, 153–56; *see also* Debt crisis; Developing countries; Financial markets; Securities

"Big Bang," United Kingdom, 153

Bilateralism, 93–95; as distinct from multilateralism, 93; *see also* Bilateral trade negotiations

Bilateral trade negotiations, 85, 86, 87, 93–95, 101, 177; effect on trading system, 94–95; as prod to multilateral process, 93–94, and subsidies, 107, 115; U.S.–Canada, 84, 93–94, 101, 163; U.S.–Mexico, 94; *see also* Bilateralism

Biotechnology, 18, 111

Brazil, 14, 16, 63, 167

Bretton Woods conference, 10, 45, 178, 179

"Bryant Amendment," 168–69

Budget deficit, U.S., 6, 11, 13, 20–34, 38, 41, 42*n.6*, 54, 105, 174, 180; as a constraint on U.S. economic policymaking, 5, 13, 26, 29, 34; effect on foreign aid, 76, 77; qualitatively and quantitatively different during Reagan years, 174; and savings rate, 174; and social security surplus, 26–27, 33; *see also* Budget deficit reduction

Budget deficit reduction, U.S., 5, 20–34, 37, 40–41, 42*n.9*, 58, 105, 129–30, 174–76, 185–86; and agriculture programs, 30; and burden-sharing, 34–37; as a constraint on new government programs, 26; and credibility abroad, 24, 33–34, 40, 180; and defense spending, 24, 25, 27–29, 32–33, 176; effect on world economy, 39, 41; in an expanding economy, 25; and entitlement expenditures, 24, 27, 29–30, 33, 176; on expenditure side, 27–30, 32–33, 40, 176; and foreign aid, 30; and foreign debt service, 27, 33, 41, 54; interest rates and, 27, 33, 129–30; and new labor adjust-

235

About the Authors

C. Michael Aho is director of economic studies and director of the International Trade Project at the Council on Foreign Relations in New York. He holds a Ph.D. in economics from the Massachusetts Institute of Technology and an undergraduate degree from the University of Michigan. Before joining the Council in 1984, Aho was the economic policy advisor to Senator Bill Bradley (1983–84); director of the Office of Foreign Economic Research at the U.S. Department of Labor (1978–82); and U.S. representative to the Manpower and Social Affairs Committee of the OECD (1981–82). He directed the *President's Report on U.S. Competitiveness, 1980*, has published widely on trade and labor adjustment issues, including as co-author of *Trade Talks: America Better Listen!* (Council on Foreign Relations, 1985), and is a frequent contributor to the media.

Marc Levinson is editorial director of *The Journal of Commerce* in New York. He holds a Master's degree in public and international affairs from the Woodrow Wilson School at Princeton University; a Master's degree in government administration from Georgia State University; and an undergraduate degree from Antioch College in Ohio. Previously, Levinson was senior editor of the *Business Month* (formerly *Dun's Business Month*), a staff correspondent for the Bureau of National Affairs, Inc., and a reporter for *Time*. Levinson has written extensively on economic issues for a wide variety of magazines, and is author of *Beyond Free Markets: The Revival of Activist Economics* (Lexington Books, 1988).